FAIRY TALES ARE TRUE

SILENT REACH FROM THE DUNES TO THE KUMBHA MELA

SHAMCHER BRYN BEORSE

THE SHAMCHER ARCHIVES

ALPHA GLYPH PUBLICATIONS

Fairy Tales are True
Silent Reach from the Dunes to the Kumbha Mela
©1978 Shamcher Bryn Beorse and © 2014 The Shamcher
Archives
Introduction © 2014 by Carol Sill

ISBN: 978-0-9783485-5-7

CIP data available on request

Cover Design: Diane Feught
www.fairy-tales.shamcher.com

Alpha Glyph Publications Ltd.
Vancouver BC Canada
www.alphaglyph.com

FAIRY TALES ARE TRUE

CONTENTS

Introduction

Welcome to the world in which fairy tales are true, where the prominent scientists of the day join together to seek wisdom from a great sage of the Himalayas at the fabled Kumbha Mela. Guided by a trusted myth-spinning storyteller, their journey and its preparation are peppered with tales of metaphysical adventures. From the bohemian Shangri-La of the Oceano Dunes to the ancient Ganges flowing from Himalayan heights, the group travels and discovers the realm of "silent reach".

In the tradition of metaphysical fiction that was popular in the 1920's and 30s, *Fairy Tales are True* sweeps the reader into a vortex of yogis, scientists, spies and fools. Unlike most of those forgotten novels of secret universal Buddhist brotherhoods and mystical Tibetan quests, this book is more than partly true. Bryn Beorse, who was known to the Sufis as Shamcher, was the real deal: an actual world-travelling yogi-sufi who also was an esteemed economist and engineer. Here he has created a fantastical autobiographical allegory in a book that defies categorization.

As one long teaching story comprised of nested teaching stories, Beorse's book may take liberties with facts to illustrate truths, but not as often as you might think. It is not only autobiographical, it is also a novelized or storified account of concepts that cannot be easily grasped by the literal mind.

Many-faceted, the book can be seen as a comic or as an allegory, as a novel or as a collection of stories like *1001 Nights*, as an autobiography or as a metaphysical encryption, all depending on your viewpoint.

Some of the astonishing tales are completely true, other more prosaic events may be literary fabrication. Some facts are condensed and seen as averages. Other events resonate a mythic dimension or parallel in which they become more than true.

Shamcher often said that we need to create new myths and he shows the way here by generating myths from real-life experiences. The myth of the union of the sciences, the myth of the free-living dunites, the myth of mystic Indian sages beaming integrating love-wisdom. These new myths become outlines for humanity to decode.

This book is a cycle of words and letters set to run as a sort of intuition-machine – generating insights in the reader who can approach it from the right angle, at the right time.

Our story begins in a shattering of the separation between disciplines and points of view. With a gunshot, the "burglars" break the barriers and enter one another's realms of exploration. Breaking the sound barrier naturally causes a sonic boom. In one big *Bang!* the action begins, and characters, events and social/political situations all combine to seek the whereabouts of a secret being who draws them together.

As science writer Brian Clegg states, "Every point in the universe, including where you are right now, is where the big bang happened."

The book's characters and situations could be seen as cliché, but just as McLuhan observed, cliché expands into archetype.

Shamcher sketches a series of event patterns that demonstrate the action and effect of what he calls "silent reach." In these narrative examples of communication without words, silent reach shows in the mental concentration shared by three yogis to save the life of a foolhardy swimmer in the Ganges. It is seen in a last-minute intervention in a drama of international relationships played out as a personal conflict in the *Tale of Fu Kieng*. Silent reach, throughout the book, leads up to an inspired integration of the disciplines in the presence of a mysterious sage.

Ranging from the highest physics to the social sciences, Beorse has created exemplars, characters partly based on actual scientists. They are the noble knights of France, America and England setting forth upon their quest, with the guidance of the troubadour, our storytelling narrator. Dr. Jacques and his Institute – all true, except his last name was not Miel but Ménétrier. He figures in several of Shamcher's other books, including *Planet Earth Demands* and *Every Willing Hand*. Edmund Fitzgerald seems to be a composite character based on prominent innovative social scientists and economists of the day (with a dash of Beorse himself.)Sir James Oss is patterned on Sir James Jeans the eminent physicist, astronomer and mathematician. By creating a confluence of these great minds of the early and mid-20th century, Beorse is working a little bit of magic.

Shamcher gives to the boy who could see without eyes the name of one of India's greatest poets, a man who learned the inner secret of the shared mind of all. When Rabindranath (the blind and simple seer) tells of future wonders, our engineer/narrator asks for hard facts on how to achieve the wonders on earth. The response shows delicate awareness of the process of humanity's evolution on earth and the fulfillment of such prophesy that comes slowly, over time.

As an engineer, Shamcher had an intimate understanding of technology, its inspiration and application for the good of all. For decades he worked to develop and promote OTEC (Ocean Thermal Energy Conversion) as a benign source of power from the sea, a system he outlined in his book, *Planet Earth Demands*. He refers to it again in his book on full employment, *Every Willing Hand*.

Interweaving teaching stories with personal accounts, Beorse brings life to ephemeral concepts. He allegorically illustrates world events, such as the influence of Chinese expansion into India in the *Tale of Fu Kieng*. Putting himself directly into the center of the most dramatic action in the book, he once again weaves in his own life experience with that of the field he wishes to illustrate. Is it factual or is it true?

The book's poetic introductory note symbolically reveals the entire work and its premise. First is the Magi: the wise one, perhaps *rassoul*, spirit of guidance, source of all beauty, creator of harmony. He travels, not only from place to place but from body to body, being to being, and time to time. It is said that he sleeps – for in all places and persons he is present, both dormant and emergent.

He is the master who brings the lions and the lambs to lay down together.

Who are these *lions*? They are no more the kings and queens of the animals, lords of the realm, symbolically referring to the rulers of this world in which we live and have our being. Today, to Shamcher, they are the physicists, who understand that there is no longer such a hierarchial world-view. The world, its meaning and scientific understanding, is in their hands to determine, decode, and interpret. Yet these ones do not know it all, no matter how advanced their "knowledge."

They do not devour the lambs, but lie down now with them. These *lambs* represent the gentle ones, the innocents, traditionally sacrificed, tender, pure, simple. Easy targets - but in the presence of the Magi they are able to be with the lions and not be eaten or sacrificed. To Shamcher, these are the sages, the wise of all time. The innocent wise whose wisdom teaches them that they, too, do not "know."

For both physicists and sages there is a great unknowing which is in fact the presence of the Magi - a vast field of super-intelligence and super-wisdom beyond all human endeavor, whether secular or spiritual. This is unknowable from both points of view. For the physicist it is incalculable. For the sage it is unknowable. Shamcher refers to this state as completely "undetermined" in the sense of the word as immeasurable or incalculable.

When the Magi sleeps with the lions and the lambs,

there is a fertilization and from the joyful womb springs creation itself. Manifestation. Perhaps the Magi does more than remain dormant in the process. Perhaps "sleeping" with the lions and the lambs is an activation, a catalyst, a love-making, a life-giving magic force. Creation springs from this communion.

And what is this joyful womb? Like the Taoist womb, out of which comes the ten thousand things, it is an unending fountain or spring continuously pouring forth, in joy, the entire created universe. Emergent, ever-growing, source of all.

Sages dedicate their lives to knowing it. It cannot be known. Physicists dedicate their lives to determining it. It cannot be determined. Yet as the outpouring is never-ending, it can be perceived, and over time, "seen" in a way – by "averages" – sensed mathematically in an overview. Words from other times refer to these "averages" as correspondences or harmonies.

Simply taking parts of the puzzle picture, putting them together and determining their average can yield the closest thing to "knowing" this creation. The Magi in the union of the lion and the lamb creates a new harmony, a new "average", an inclusive ideal that unifies all endeavours toward the one.

This book can be seen as an explication of this premise. Hot points or moments of intensity all share the common awareness or reference to the presence of the Magi, the unseen one, through the silent reach of unknowable communication which some sages have achieved. After gathering together, the sciences are led to the greatest of the sages in a journey that catalyzes them to greater realization in their fields through interdisciplinary dialogue in a very high place, guided by an unknowable presence. This is all stimulated along the way with true tales of adventures or mystery, pointing always to the silent communication of the wise.

This book is also an allegory of the life of the seeker, who gathers all forces together, with the help of a guide, to seek the truth, much like Attar's classic Sufi tale, *The Conference of the Birds*. It could be said that the whole tale occurs within each of us – the sciences, the events, the guide (our narrator) and the great one whose appearance inspires and unifies, while daily we are engaged with the surging crowds of humanity within - our own personal Kumbha Mela.

It is also significant that *Fairy Tales are True* features one of the rare accounts of life in the Dunes of Oceano, where Shamcher lived on and off during the late 1930's. Here mystics, free-thinkers, poets, painters and photographers mingled freely with drifters and others on the fringes of society, in a place so pure and beautiful it was photographed over and over again by Ansel Adams, Edward Weston and many others.

Those iconic American images were not inspired simply by sand dunes alone, but by the remarkable community there, many of whose members were very engaged in silent reach and fairy tales. The loosely connected group called the "dunites" was expanded and stimulated by the astrologer Gavin Arthur (grandson of US President Chester Arthur). Here the Irish mystical folklorist and friend of the Faeries, Ella Young, named Gavin's cabin *Moy Mell* (after the poets' Pasture of Honey in the Gaelic afterlife). From that center, and many dinner parties later, was birthed the *Dune Journal*, a short-lived radical magazine discussing art, nature, economics, astrology, nudism, architecture, and mysticism. All this and more were created in this atmosphere of Bohemia and Shangri-la in the Dunes of California. Much of Shamcher's description of the Dunes is true, with only a few names changed and situations condensed. "Irma" was actually the dunite Dixie Paul. "Dreamwood" also really existed: he was the artist and dunite Elwood Decker. "Hugo" is the poet and early dunite, Hugo Seelig. Moon Mullins, and many more are mentioned here by name.

Bringing with him the legacy of Whitman and Carpenter, Gavin Arthur openly embraced life in loving compassion, nurturing an independent, inspiring and stimulating environment for all who wished to participate. Later, in San Francisco, he helped nurture counterculture through the decades of both the beat and hippie movements.

During the Great Depression, economic theories were hotly debated in the dunes, forging a new way of thinking. Not confined to only socialism and communism, active discussion of new concepts ranged through Social Credit, barter and Shamcher's giro-credit, and other economic innovations. In the early-mid 1930's Shamcher's well-received economic book, *Distribute or Destroy,* had been published, first in Norway and then in the US. It was quoted in a book by sometime dunites Luther Whiteman and Samuel L. Lewis, *Glory Roads: The Psychological State of California.* Contact with Whiteman brought the Dunes into Shamcher's awareness and he soon showed up there and settled in.

Whiteman's satirical book, *The Face of the Clam,* was a simplistic look at the phenomenon of dune living that didn't positively reflect the Dune community. In *Fairy Tales are True*, Shamcher corrects the balance, diffusing reactions to this book and how the community felt about it.

In the late 1920's and 30s the coast of California was dotted with spiritual communities, temples and metaphysical groups, each dedicated to alternative lifestyles and usually devoted to the founder. Devotees worked, dowagers donated, and a network of nodes for the coming "Age of Aquarius" was begun. But none was more radical and free than the Oceano Dunes, which required nothing at all from anyone who wished to join in the dunite way of life.

The dunes were a place of total independence and self sufficiency. Some dunites were social, others were hermits, never seen for weeks or months, either meditating or hiding from the law. It was the perfect place to disappear from the world. This utopian community of radical individuals was a decentralized independent association of hermits and hermeticists, of yogis and boogeymen.

The dunes hosted gaelic rituals, nudism, visiting dignitaries, artists, writers, meditators, curiosity seekers. At sunrise, some dunites stood at the edge of the sea chanting "Lemuria, Lemuria," willing the mythic island continent to rise again. It might seem to be a fabrication that narrow-minded spiritual seekers in the dunes received inner mis-guidance to burn away evil by burning down someone's cabin, but in fact this is a part of dune history. In reality, it was burnt to the ground and then rebuilt, better than before.

Nearby Halcyon had been a Theosophical community,

while, closer to the dunes, the little town of Oceano later boasted Gavin Arthur's Hill House, where he lived when not at Moy Mell in the dunes. Here many parties with the intellectual and artistic elite of the day left dunites wandering home under the stars, a little (or a lot) tipsy and drunk with ideas. In fog or when no moon reflected from the clamshells placed on roofs and the old pavilion pylons, a dunite could easily be lost in the dark of night with only the sounds of the sea or the frogs to follow.

The extensive section *Tale of the Sanyassin and the Dunes* is a further expansion of Beorse's technique – taking his own life experience, adding a bit of history and a layer of myth to deepen the scope. Naming Ménétrier "Miel" gives him a home in Moy Mell, the Pasture of Honey in the dunes, which itself is a name for the poet's heaven "where the spirits dwell."

Does the tale take over from the facts? It is up to each of us to see, like blind Rabindranath, not with the eyes but with intuition.

"What do you think of the New Age?" someone once asked Shamcher.

"It might be new to you," he quipped in reply.

Over and over again Shamcher emphasizes the power of communicating without words. His ability to do just that was one of his remarkable qualities. His being was a locus of energies and forces which urged, emerged and converged within him. Not only did he have access to the minds of others, and areas of interest created through merged minds of scientists, and engineers, and economists, he had access to the great mind of the entire being of humanity, the earth and our whole human experiment. Through Sufi yoga he attained awareness and flexibility to play in this vast God-mind, and through his loving heart he connected with other souls who could, perhaps, understand.

As a servant of this great mind Shamcher did its bidding without hesitation and he remained in contact at all times toward the end of his life. This inner urge and direct guidance was for him a force of great loving action. He said that the further you go in this way, the greater the minds you swing with. He was not only referring to remarkable people with fine gifts and abilities, but he also meant fields of awareness – physics, cosmologies, religions, beings of all life – animals and plants and unseen life. All "minds," all aware and communicating silently.

This deceptively simple and slim volume could be seen as a blueprint for experience, for the book invokes a natural participation from the universe. It can amplify our awareness of quantum entanglement, what Einstein referred to as "spooky action at a distance." There are mythic tropes that Beorse expands upon, such as the effects of yogic concentration or the sacred unification of the sciences. Intuition stimulated through the lens of this book may awaken a recognition of such event templates as quantum patterns, living symbols that could seem to leap off the page and into everyday reality. *The Tale of Trailanga* is echoed in Dreamwood's arrest, but it is not confined to this novel. It is also echoed in the story of Big Bear, an aboriginal shaman arrested in Winnipeg during the Metis rebellion in Canada. He too could not be confined; his story is one of several that mirror Trailanga's, despite separation in both time and place.

When Shamcher wrote this book in the late 1960s-70s, he placed some of the action in decades past. The original book description read:

> *From California pre-hippy communes of forty years ago, to the mysterious convening of the sages in modern-day India, this story sweeps the reader along following the secret thread whose strands have held mankind together for the last few thousand years. Visits to simple villagers with amazing powers alternate with the adventures of an expedition of the world's most important scientists, as Bryn Beorse takes us into the "inner sanctums" of our own everyday world.*

The inner journey is reflected here as outer. The signs along the path all point to the silent way. We sense and discover it through stories that map the way and help encourage faith in the unseen.

As Shamcher said in the book, "If the great one wished to see us, he would somehow arrange it."

Reading this book intuitively can reveal a deeper symbolic truth - something ultimately even more direct than a tale of scientists and sages working together to understand the truth of our existence and the meaning of the cosmos. As this compendium of nested teaching tales was intuitively written, it can speak to the heart of each reader in the silent reach of communication beyond words.

Carol Sill, Vancouver BC, 2014

The magi travels. He sleeps with the lions and the lambs. The lions are the physicists who know that they don't know. The lambs are the sages who know that they don't know. Out of the joyful womb springs creation, unknown, undetermined, except for averages.

The Journey Begins

Our talk had rambled on through the night, when Jacques Miel, the Parisian with that honey voice, broke into Shakespeare,

"But soft! What light through yonder window breaks?"

Had a new idea dawned? Or only a new day, just then breaking through the diamond-shaped window panes, multicoloring the solid mahogany desk — comfortably cluttered with Tibetan masks, shrunken Dayak heads, unlit pipes, penciled scribblings and leatherbound books.

Behind that desk sat Edward Fitzgerald, our gracious host. He paused and acknowledged the interruption — and the daylight — and then continued, "…until what we have left is no less than a synthesis of all human knowledge."

Sir James Oss coughed disapprovingly, "Now Edward, I'm reminded once more that your behavioral sciences have always been more grandiose than my humble physics."

"And to prove it….," hissed Fitzgerald, rising briskly, kicking his chair back, whipping a gun from his pocket, aiming high, pulling the trigger. An ear-splitting BANG underlined his words, "We are *burglars* today, Jim, breaking into each other's sacred circles. Common criminals…"

Sir James had watched this performance with neither excitement nor approval. He bowed down, gripped the end of the little rug Fitzgerald was standing on, and pulled. The sociologist came down with a crash.

"A common criminal should at least make sure where he stands," flashed Sir James.

The door burst open and all eyes turned to take in an exciting view: wild curls bobbing around shapely shoulders, flashing through frightened eyes fixed on the figure on the floor. Adorable lips curled to spew anxious words, "Oh my God! I thought I heard a shot! Gerald, what happened?"

Fitzgerald turned his head and announced from his prone position, "Gentlemen, may I introduce Dr. Jane Weiner, this university's and the world's new mathematical wizard."

"To a Frenchman," intoned Jacques Miel, with an accent to match, "it appears incomprehensible to introduce such a sublime specimen from a respectless, supine position. And he even broke the rule of a lady's first right to know. So allow me. This is physicist Sir James Oss of the distinguished University of Edinburgh, and I am a simple medic, Jacques Miel, of the Sorbonne."

"Speaking of the devil," said Fitzgerald, still on his back, "isn't Jacques the arch-criminal though? Isn't his 'International Center for Scientific Research' simply an intellectual Mafia? This monster covers thinkers and tinkerers from every branch, every cult of science, and it can think, plan and attack in the realms of medicine, physics, biochemistry, psychiatry, economics — with the power of a thousand-armed octopus. In the inner, secret nub of this web sits our arch-hood, Jacques Miel!"

Jacques turned to Jane. "We owe you an explanation. The shot you heard, and our gracious host's supine position. He wanted to impress us all with the crossing of the barriers, the breaking into our respective circles, the committing of burglaries, by bangs and crashes, if necessary, the violent communication between the closets of science. However, he hadn't made sure what he was standing on. Sir James helped him see."

"I like it down here," protested Fitzgerald. "I can see you all from a different angle. And my pride? Good riddance."

"About time," sighed Sir James.

"My mathematics," Jane Weiner began, "was once called the Queen of Science, proof and criteria of all knowledge. Now come my mentors, Eric Bell, Kurt Goedel and others, telling us there aren't any proofs, never were. Math is spun out of the human mind like the web of a spider and is not an existing structure, waiting for discovery."

Sir James nodded approvingly. "When Schrodinger and Einstein wrapped your equations around the universe or its parts, we had second thoughts. There is topology, for example. You draw a neat figure on a rubber sheet and then pull and twist the sheet and take a new and sober look at the figure which was once so neatly drawn. From this, Einstein obtains his new version of what Newton called gravity. The body isn't pulled at all. It just moves over a wrinkle, over a mathematical mountainside. But does it, really?"

Jane, meanwhile, was looking around the room at each face. Her eyes fell on me, with well-bred bewilderment.

We had not even been introduced. Why should we have been? Who was I, anyway? What business did I have in this august company? I appraised myself lucky to be an inconsequential observer.

Jane suppressed her wish to ask who the hell I was, and she spoke. "Einstein successfully tore us loose from Newton's concept. Now why would anyone follow this new prophet into other rigid ideas?"

"And so?" Fitzgerald was impatient with any loquaciousness but his own.

"So we are wary of pretty pictures," responded Jane. "Look at our electronics. Nobody knows what is behind these wonders. And do we care? But we work with our haphazard discoveries. Will we ever understand? Perhaps, when we have crossed the time barrier, the pride barrier, the nostalgic memory barrier, the science slang barrier..."

The door burst open again and three young men stumbled in, "Was anybody shot?"

Fitzgerald, still in his supine position, shook his head.

"My brave security force, all that happened here during the time you patiently waited outside, fearing to get involved, was just some demonstration of academic burglary, in the course of which I lost my footing – we have to keep up with television, you know – but say, what were *you* doing all this time?"

The three looked at each other, "Eh – we have to keep up with television too, don't we?"

Miel nodded as the threesome left; then spoke, "Remember how we once breathlessly absorbed the fairy tale about brilliant men building ever new and solid bricks into a formidable structure of science? This present generation is tearing down this structure brick by brick."

Sir James nodded, "We have modern Platos, then Einsteins, and Frisches. Like Plato some think what our senses or instruments record are merely shadows of the real world. I respect these people. They may even be right.

"But they have placed themselves outside science, which does not ponder what is inaccessible The Einsteins, Schrodingers, Whiteheads wait in reverence for the perfection of the Quantum Theory to show us and prove to us every detail of existence. They look simply for refinement in our methods of observation.

"The Otto Frisches, along with most of us today, do not look for simple, finite 'solutions.' Every observation acts on the observer, if only by the impact of a single light quantum.

"The 'objective outside world' is not objective, not outside. It is a product of our own minds, suited to the observer's particular network. Yes, we should seek a synthesis."

"I am with you, Sir James, all the way," said Fitzgerald.

"While I am not any longer," said Jane Weiner. "You begin to sound more and more like science fiction, Sir James."

Sir James blushed awkwardly.

"Why, Sir James, really?" said Jane. "Don't tell me you read that stuff?"

Fitzgerald laughed. "He doesn't read it. He writes it. I'm sure that you, distinguished lady, and you, distinguished gentlemen, have never heard of Astra, the brightest star of the comic strip firmament."

Sir James coughed. His face was growing redder.

"Well," said Fitzgerald, hugely enjoying Sir James' discomfort, "And Astra's creator is none other than the eminent Sir James Oss."

Sir James dabbed at his face with a handkerchief and then carefully returned it to his pocket.

"If I need to defend myself, my science fiction originated before my status in science, when I was just a boy and tried to orient myself in this contradictory world. That was long before science fiction became a craft.

"I wrote fantasies about the universe and man and his destiny and our sisters and brothers on other planets. It was on the basis of these speculations that I decided to become a scientist, patiently probing for the truth.

"Of course, I was delighted when, at long last, my fantasies became a product which would sell. Now, my science fiction is not only an outlet for thoughts not yet ripe for scientific journals, but it is also a source of extra income which has paid for many of the instruments which, day by day, bring us closer to my boyhood dreams."

"What particularly interests me about science fiction," said Dr. Jacques in his melodious voice, "is that it has made acceptable to a large segment facts and feats long realized — not necessarily by aliens from other planets, but by hermits, sages, Yogis, Sufis and other simple geniuses here on earth. What Americans and Europeans would not believe of their own species, they readily accept when applied to interstellar beings."

Sir James nodded. "I have often thought that our dreams of mastery of life and death, psychic powers, invulnerability and so forth, expressed in our science fiction may stem from memories of past achievements of our own race, or from half-conscious communications with adepts existing here on earth."

Jane Weiner shook her head in consternation. "You amaze me. Edward suggested that our common ambition was to break into each other's minds and I agreed. I came here with sufficient respect for you gentlemen to want to share your knowledge. But now, I'm not so sure.

"Sir James Oss, my ideal in the realm of physical science, has turned out to be a dabbler in science fiction, the hash which is about to destroy the sobriety of our youth.

"And now, worse, Sir James and Dr. Jacques both come out for the yogis and mystics – charlatans living off the credulity of uneducated people – phonies who have been debunked a thousand times over."

Dr. Jacques looked at Jane as only a Frenchman can. "Our charming mathematician is right," he said. "Yogis and mystics have been found wanting time and again and thousands more will fail the test. But there is one point to consider," he paused for emphasis, "A counterfeit is, after all, made from a pattern."

"Your point, of course, is that phony mystics prove that genuine ones exist," said Jane. "But if they do, where do they keep themselves? Have you ever seen one?"

"Where would you keep yourself if you were one?" asked Dr. Jacques.

"Available," said Jane passionately. "Available to the sick and needy, available to science, so that my faculties could be registered and investigated and repeated, if possible."

"In that sense," said Dr. Jacques, "I'd say that they are available. They are available to the sick and needy who do not need to see them in order to benefit. They are available to the people who are willing to give their whole lives to studying them and repeating their feats.

"But they are not available to lightweight scientists who thoughtlessly invade their intricate worlds with inadequate theories and instruments, leaving a trail of confusion. They are not available to the curious who would mob them, to the show people who would first exploit them and then destroy them or to the envious who would strangle them. For people with such talents, there is little choice but to hide."

"Hide?" said Jane. "Where?"

"There are two ways of hiding," replied Dr. Jacques. "A simple way and a subtle way. (A geographical way and a personal way.) Some of my friends have, in remote areas, stumbled onto hermits who can almost stop their hearts, who take no food, who communicate with friends without words. Near the Gangotri Glaciers, for example, in the upper Himalayas, beyond the shrines of Badrinath and Kedernath, in places untenable to any human needing food and shelter."

"But why should they hide in such outrageous places?" asked Jane.

"Why not?" said Dr Jacques, shrugging. "If they communicate freely at any distance, they have no need of close company. If they do not eat, except for, perhaps, a pinch of crushed rock for mineral supply, they have no need for farm land. They have no craving or need for palaces or huts or any shelter at all.

"But a more subtle way to hide is in a crowd. Such people hide, not their bodies, but their powers. There is the story of an Indian peasant, for example, known to others in his village as a pious, humble, simple soul. He had a son with vision and ambition who went far away to Tibet and came home, after many years of study, a man of many talents.

"Among other things, he had learned how to walk on water. Proudly, he started to show his simple, ignorant father how he could walk across the foaming river which passed near the village. He was halfway across when the swirling water frightened him. He fell and would have drowned had not his father calmly walked out and picked him out of the water and carried him to shore."

Dr Jacques looked around the group, smiling. "The young man was amazed. 'Father!' he exclaimed. 'I did not know you could do that.'

"The old man replied, 'My son, that is the difference between us. You know many things and I know nothing at all, except what is required of me.'"

Jane shook her head. "That is a very pretty story, Dr. Jacques. And now I am beginning to understand something Edward said earlier. That you wanted us to discuss a possible journey. I suppose you want us to go visit this simple peasant."

"No, Jane," said Dr. Jacques, "He would show us nothing, tell us nothing. But we do have an invitation." He inclined his head toward me. "From our quiet friend."

"Another science fiction writer, no doubt," said Jane, smiling at me to take the sting out of her words.

"Not even that," I said. "Not even a Ph.D. I am just a

nobody and I claim to be nothing else."

I smiled at Jane Weiner. "I travel extensively in the Far East and I have come here to offer myself as your guide to the Kumbha Mela."

"Kumbha Mela? What is the Kumbha Mela?" asked Jane.

"It's a sort of fair, Miss Weiner. An occurrence very twelve years when the holy men come down out of their hiding places and mingle with the populace. A sort of pilgrimage in reverse."

"And you expect to meet some remarkable person at this Kumbha Mela," said Jane Weiner.

"Yes," I answered. "At least, I hope to. One can never be sure, but my expectations are great."

Sir James Oss had been watching and listening to my exchange with Jane Weiner and now he laughed quietly and said, "Well, I shan't argue with you. Count me in. This is the sort of thing I like to be in on. Something indefinite, unsure, like my doubts before my instruments, like my childhood speculations. And, like them, holding great promise. This is full of the only attitude which can possibly bring up anything new. And the idea of such a trip arranged by a nobody."

He paused and smiled at me. "With all due respect, sir, I'm overwhelmed with the privilege of just meeting an honest nobody. Such a rarity. Such a gem."

"And I am with you," said Edward Fitzgerald enthusiastically. "I have long wished to study the behavior patterns of a factual nobody. Not to mention Sir James' reaction to one."

Dr. Jacques turned the attention of the group back to Jane Weiner. "And what about Miss Mathematician?"

She looked soberly and somewhat chidingly at the group. "I shall stay home, thank you, and be prepared to listen sympathetically when you return to tell about the big one that got away."

Dr. Jacques sighed, "I had been counting above all on your charming company, my dear Jane. And your critical mind. When I was young and enterprising, you know, ladies had intuition, not mind. Today they have mind, but, unfortunately, I am not sure they still have intuition."

"Thank you, Dr. Jacques," she said. "But it just might be my intuition which tells me not to waste good working days."

Dr. Jacques spoke to her seriously. "Your intuition, if you still had it, dear Jane, would not necessarily have encouraged belief in hermits with great powers, but it would certainly have looked up when I told the story of the humble father and his son. For this is a story rich in the subtle language of symbology.

"It is a message about the riches of experience gained through a humble life as against tricks learned during a spurt of hurried ambition. To the intuitive, the details fade against the deep, symbolic truth. Then, when the sensitive tentacles of intuition would go on to ponder the possibility of actually walking on water, there would just be a suspension of judgment. Intuition does not care. It does not affirm, nor does it deny, in any case where there is no experience."

"But don't you see that this trip would be just a waste

of time for me?" said Jane.

"Perhaps. Perhaps not."

Dr. Jacques paused and smiled at her.

"Remember that no one wants to convince you of anything. None of us go because we believe or want to believe. We go to see and listen and perhaps learn."

"Yes, Jane," said Sir James Oss.

"Your firmness appears to me to be a weakness. You took the great step of sweeping away the apparently solid foundation of mathematics, guided by Bell, Goedel and others, but this one step seems to have overawed you. Now you insist upon staying up in your niche of nothing. But why not continue to look around? To see and make sure that you are right?"

Edward Fitzgerald looked at Jane with hostly concern. "If you are not coming with us, Miss Mathematics, we shall feel duty bound to report to you after the event so that you can put our findings into the proper equations."

'Thank you, Edward. Thank you all," said Jane. "And I wish you the best of luck."

She smiled. "You may be surprised to know that I do know a little of the 'mystic lore of the inscrutable East' myself. My roommate when I was an undergraduate was an incurable romantic and a budding mystic.

"I remember her telling me about the Himalayan musk deer. With the scent of musk in his nostrils, the animal becomes obsessed and rushes through the woods, jumps across streamlets and sometimes leaps to his death over a cliff in a frantic search for the source of the fervid fragrance."

She looked around at all of us and then continued. "But all the time, the musk for which it searched so madly was hidden it its own body."

She looked at us once again and then said, "My roommate is now a dowdy housewife in Plainfield, New Jersey."

She smiled around at all of us once more and began gathering her things, preparing to go.

I felt a strange disappointment and a sense of failure that she was not going to accompany us, but before I could marshal my thoughts and attempt to persuade her further, she was gone.

The next days were full of preparations for the journey.

The three famous men went about putting their affairs in order for their absences, and I busied myself with the mundane details of the trip. But almost every night we met at Edward Fitzgerald's and, after disposing of any business having to do with the journey, we talked. Or rather, I talked, usually, because the three of them were very eager to hear as much about my experiences in the East as possible.

THE TALE OF RABINDRANATH AND PAURI

I came to know Rabindranath Rao while I was on an assignment in the Garwhal district of the Himalayas. His father, Pauri Rao, came to see me every evening after working his plot of land across the Lake of Heavenly Fulfillment.

Pauri's eight children had the grace and suppleness of the hill folk, but their eyes were sore and their bellies bloated from malnutrition. I gave him bottles of vitamins for them and these he accepted. But I could not make him accept gifts of canned foods. His people ate only curried vegetables in reverence to the sacred shrines in the area.

Pauri's neighbors told me that he was a descendant of the fierce Rajput princes. I was not surprised, having noted his excellent manners and ever-exploring mind.

He loved to talk about the mountains and about the trees and plants and the mosses which sometimes grew and thrived even under ice and snow. He spoke feelingly about the eagles and hawks and the musk deer. And he spoke often of the rishis and yogis and their philosophies and their alleged achievements, such as an instant healing and knowing a man's thoughts at any distance.

Then, in a different voice, he would go on to talk

of Rabindranath, his youngest child. The boy's name, inherited from India's great poet, was not amiss, for little Rabindranath had a poet's vision, even though he was blind.

"God took away his sight so that his soul might see," said his proud, but humble father.

There had been a time when Rabindranath could only listen to the tales others brought him, about the trees and leaves and flowers, about the wide meadow, about the luminous depths of the Lake of Heavenly Fulfillment and the blue mountains far beyond.

His father had taught him the subtle art of continuous gratitude and never to clog his mind with self-pity. So Rabindranath marveled at the beautiful world he began to see in his imagination as the others spoke. He did not know that he was adding, from his own generous heart, to the beauty they described. He did not know, at first, that he could see or sense a greater world.

But in time, when boys and girls from neighboring farms came to see Rabindranath, it was he who spoke and they who listened. Sometimes he would reach out his hand and touch one of the boys or girls, for he had also become a healer. He could sense the scars and silent cries and reach out in response.

Pauri told me all this, many times over, and I visited his home and saw the boy alone and with his friends. I knew that I was expected to say something more than polite sounds of amazement and approval, so I told Pauri about Irma Clark.

The Tale of Irma Clark

Irma lived in the dunes with her three children. This was remarkable in itself because the dunes were a man's world. Occasionally, a woman lived there for a while, but Irma was the only mother with children ever to inhabit the dunes.

The dunes I speak of lie between Santa Maria River and Oceano, "the little town on the Pacific." Irma lived in a driftwood shack which had been built years ago by moonshiners.

Each morning, Irma took the children to school in a jeep which she kept hidden among the dunes. One morning when she and the children approached the jeep, two strange men were trying to wire the ignition to start it. Without hesitation, Irma whipped out the pistol she carried and fired at them. The bullet lifted one of the men's hats and they scurried off into the dunes. When she parked the jeep that night, Irma left a sign on it which said, "The next time, my aim will be two inches lower." Predictably, she had no more trouble.

This part of the story has no great importance except to establish that Irma Clark was not a flimsy mystical sort of woman.

When Irma returned from her morning trip to the

school, she swept the sand out of the shack, washed the dishes and chopped wood from the knotty, crooked bushes. Then she went down to the beach for clams.

While she worked, Irma sang. The words were strange and sung with a weird, monumental rhythm, like mountain storms followed by sunshine. I was intrigued by the songs and asked her what language she was singing. She laughed and told me that she had no idea and that she knew no language but English.

I made notes on the songs, catching the sounds on paper as best I could, and eventually brought my notes to the Far Eastern section of the University of California where scholars looked them over. Similarities to Tibetan dialects existed, but the words, as sung by Irma, still made no sense.

Finally, the notes were sent on to a scholar in Lhasa who was a student of ancient Tibetan dialects. After a while, the Tibetan scholar wrote back that Irma's songs were perfect renditions of a long-dead Tibetan dialect.

Back to Pauri and Rabindranath

Pauri nodded calmly when my story was finished. "Of course," he said. "Our small, frail bodies are but pin-points in the vast, limitless soul which reaches out in wider and wider flames of wisdom as we delve deeper and deeper into it – the soul of all and of all time. A flash of the All-Soul overflowed into your Irma Clark's heart. From the point of view of the informed, it is not a remarkable thing at all."

My story of Irma Clark obviously was not a worthy counterpart to the phenomenon of his little blind boy, so I launched into physics. Protons, neutrons, mesons, even electrons seemed due for further subdivisions. Would this continual division of matter into smaller and smaller energy bundles bring us down to thoughts and feelings as parts of electrons and neutrons directing them? Was this the explanation of Rabindranath's insight and power? Would statistical mathematics help us solve our problems of the soul as it had helped in nuclear physics?

I linked my question with bits of Bergstrom's dream theories and Freud's depth psychology. My real intention was to impress upon this man that we had thinkers in the West also.

Pauri nodded appreciatively, but still did not seem

much impressed. Then he reverted to his favorite theme.

"My Rabindranath says men will come and tell us of even greater wonders. Of houses and palaces built from thought forms. Of a whole civilization of ease and beauty."

"Do you mean that they will come and tell about such things without showing how they can be done?" I asked him.

I could not keep myself from baiting him. Dreams were all right if they were recognized as such. But confusion between dream and reality upset my engineering mind.

Pauri smiled indulgently. "Oh, the doers will come later," he said. "The talkers come first to prepare the ground, to warn people to be alert and expectant. And some of the listeners will believe firmly enough to achieve. The talkers will make doers of dreamers. They fire the imagination so that others will dream the prophecies into fulfillment. For even now, today, there are powerful minds among us, hidden, living under insignificant circumstances because they do not know or remember their own power."

He paused and then, instead of turning the conversation back to his son, asked me a startling thing. "Tell me about your religion," he said.

I was embarrassed. "My religion? Why every sincere religion is my religion."

"Of course," he answered patiently. "But tell me about that one sincere religion in which you were brought up."

"Really," I said. "You would do better to talk to a missionary."

"I would rather hear it from a non-professional. One whom the religion was meant to help."

So I began, fumbling. As the story developed, I became engrossed in it myself, more than I had thought possible for an engineer who had been out of touch for a long time with all this. I glanced at Pauri. He sat as if transfixed, but noticed my look.

"Before," he said, "you were talking with the pride of your mind. Now you are released into the ocean of wisdom."

I went on. When I came to the story of the Genezerath Sea and the stilling of the storm and the walking on the water, Pauri's eyes were wide and full of light.

When I finished, he said, "Tell all that again."

I did and then, in an aura of wonderment and awe, he rose and went to his home.

When a week had passed and Pauri had not come back, I was sure that my story about "the religion I had been brought up in" had somehow misfired. I castigated myself for playing the part of the busybody missionary even though he had insisted. I felt that I would never see him again.

On an evening, over a week later, I was sitting with my back to the Lake of Heavenly Fulfillment, watching an incredible purple and gold sunset and brooding over my loss of Pauri when his voice startled me. I turned and saw him and his son, Rabindranath.

"Sahib," said Pauri, his voice full of emotion, "you have taught us to walk upon the Lake of Heavenly Fulfillment." His eyes shone. Rabindranath's face was serene and his stomach was almost normal-sized.

I looked past them at the lake. The setting sun had turned the still surface scarlet. It looked solid, like polished marble. I almost asked them to walk across it again, to show me. I even thought of trying it myself. But then I realized the futility of such a request or even such an attempt. It would have implied a doubt which would have forever spoiled our mutually trusting friendship. Even if they had tried to satisfy my wishes, my own doubt would have been reflected in them and they might have failed because of it.

I looked into Rabindranath's face. His eyes, which in others mirror the soul, were blank, but I felt as if he were looking at me with a thousand eyes.

Words of James Jeans, the physicist-philosopher, came to mind: "The twentieth century's outstanding achievement is not the theory of relativity (which is probably not final anyway) but the recognition that the motions of electrons and atoms do not resemble those of the parts of a locomotive so much as those of dancers in a cotillion!"

Rabindranath, the poorest of the poor of a poor nation, would wake in the morning with an eager, thankful appetite, ready for whatever the Good Creator would provide, not doubting that He would provide. He was the dancer in the cotillion.

"Pauri. Rabindranath," I said. "It is not I who have taught you. It is you who have been teaching me. And more than just walking upon water."

THE TALE OF THE SANYASSIN IN THE DUNES

On another night, while sipping brandy in Fitzgerald's study, I told of the Sanyassin.

Between the Santa Maria River and the village of Oceano is a world of desolate sand, or so it seems from the outside. The western edge of the area referred to as "the dunes" is bounded by row upon row of tireless breakers, whipped by sand storms, whispering, mumbling and roaring. East from the sea stretch the dunes, seeming as empty and inhospitable as the wastes of the Sahara. But within these bleak hills are hidden areas of fresh green foliage and flowers and numerous small lakes.

Near the shore of one of the lakes, there is a low-slung cabin with a huge window pane at one end. A goat is usually nibbling at the shrubbery around the cabin while casting covetous eyes on a fenced-in vegetable garden. This substantial driftwood dwelling is the center and the throne of the dune kingdom – Dreamwood's cabin.

The inhabitants of the dunes are called "dunites". They are men, and sometimes women, who, for a variety of reasons, have drifted into this dune paradise and become squatters.

Some of the dunites are hiding from a wife or a husband or a sheriff. Some are extremely conscientious objectors. Others simply wish to meditate upon the vagaries of the world and the wonders of the spirit. A few, like myself, come to the dunes driven by an irrepressible curiosity and a shortage of rent money.

In my day in the dunes, Dreamwood enjoyed tremendous respect as the senior dunite. No one could remember the dunes when he was not there. And what better place could there be for an abstract painter to forget the rigid forms of the world and concentrate upon his own vision of the world?

There were times, however, when the grocer in Oceano wondered whether the blobs and shades of Dreamwood's paintings, which adorned his walls, were adequate recompense for the bread and butter and cheese and eggs delivered to the pier for Dreamwood to pick up.

The delivery of his groceries to the pier was to save Dreamwood from encountering the heavy worldly vibrations of the town of Oceano and its inhabitants, for he was a yogi, precariously perched in his own tinsel world of vibrations. When the delivery boy was safely out of sight and the tide was high, precluding car visitors on the beach, the Yogi Dreamwood drifted spirit-like to the pier and then away to his cabin with his parcel in his arms.

At the time when my story begins, the grocer was strongly considering refusing to accept any more of Dreamwood's abstracts. Just at that time, like a sacred sign from some yogi heaven, a perfect solution materialized. I happened to be the catalyst.

I was on the beach early in the morning when I saw a lone clammer. He worked with skill and speed and, as

I approached him, I admired his measured, rhythmic movements and his trim, lean body. He nodded and smiled and I saw that he had an intelligent, sensitive face, glowing with health. He looked like a fine specimen of a college athlete who had not neglected his studies.

"Do you know of a place where I can cook these clams?" he asked.

"Sure," I answered, "Come along."

He picked up a skindiver's suit and then we walked across the dunes to Dreamwood's cabin. He was impressed when he saw the lake and the greenery.

"You picked a good place to spend a vacation," I said.

"I think it's paradise," he said, looking around.

I was very curious as to who he was and where he came from and the like, but he asked no such questions so I kept silent.

There was smoke coming from Dreamwood's chimney and, however deep he might have been in meditation, he noticed our approach and came outside and waved us in. The stranger, after a brief and courteous greeting, went about cutting and frying his clams with as much skill as he had shown in picking them.

When we sat down to eat, Dreamwood gave us a long talk about yoga, telling us about his Indian teacher whom he had never met and talking with me about Irma Clark. She was the nearest example of genuine mysticism in Dreamwood's own experience.

I fidgeted at first, for Dreamwood's yoga lore did not usually enthrall newcomers. But our new friend nodded approvingly and told intimate details of the life of Dreamwood's teacher. And he explained Irma Clark's strange knowledge of the Tibetan dialect in such convincing terms of the space continuum that one might have suspected him of being the originator of the theorem. All the while, he looked with great interest and respect at the paintings stacked about the interior of the cabin.

"Your paintings are wonderful," he said to Dreamwood.

"My friend, the grocer, doesn't think so," said Dreamwood glumly. "At least, not any more." He told of his difficulties.

"Will the grocer take clams?" asked the stranger. "I like to catch more than I can eat. I'll give the grocer the rest in exchange for groceries for you and you can give me whatever of these wonderful paintings you can part with."

The bargain was struck and the stranger left the table and went to look at the paintings more closely.

"A Sanyassin," said Dreamwood to me after the stranger had gone to the paintings. "It's the name given in the Himalayas to a wandering, unattached saint spreading blessings wherever he goes."

The Sanyassin returned from his examination of the paintings glowing with excitement. "I'll be rich," he said. Then he inquired about the other dunites.

Dreamwood gave pungent descriptions of his hermit neighbors, the closest of whom lived a mile away. This nearest one was called Moon Mullins and was evidently a fugitive from justice.

"He's a raven, Moon is," said Dreamwood feelingly.

"A raven?" asked the stranger.

"Yes, a raven. He runs up and down the beach every morning, stealing all my driftwood."

The Sanyassin looked thoughtfully at a beautifully painted sign on Dreamwood's wall. "Meditate constantly," it read. "Remember she who chose the better part."

After a while, we took our leave of Dreamwood and walked along to Moon Mullin's cabin. He offered us tea. When Dreamwood was mentioned, his temper rose to the heat of boiling water.

"That holier-than-thou so-and-so," he said. "Do you know what he is?"

There was no beautifully painted clue in Moon's cabin so we remained silent.

"He's a raven, that's what he is," sputtered Moon.

"A raven?"

"Yes, a raven. Sneaking up and down the beach before breakfast, stealing all my driftwood."

I proudly displayed the Sanyassin to all the dunites in turn. After Moon came John, almost seven feet tall, slim, bronzed – the king of the dunes. John lived at Moy Mell with Emily, his queen.

It pleased me that I had had a hand in this arrangement. Like all of us, John had lived simply in a dune shack. Emily came to visit him there and in due time she was with child. She was Swedish and I was Norwegian, before whose ancestors hers had fled through the woods, and so, because of this tenuous relationship, John consulted me.

I advised him that however free and easy is the relationship between the Swedish sexes, when a child is expected, marriage follows. So they were married. John will go far, being able to take advice, and further, taking it from me.

Gavin, the retired king of the dunes, who lived now in Hill House on the edge of Oceano, was delighted with their marriage and gave them Moy Mell which sported a tiled roof and a shower.

John gave a dinner at Moy Mell in honor of the Sanyassin. The main course was a roast pig, stuffed with roasted doves which were filled with almonds. This carnal extravagance was not for Dreamwood, so he came later for dessert, creamed strawberries.

John never let his queen set foot in the kitchen and did not seem to be there much himself. In the middle of a sentence, he might slide through the doorway, as if bored with some literary horror we were discussing. (He had been a literary critic in London, where, as he put it, he had spent his life "not behind bars, but in bars, which is infinitely worse.") After a time, John would reappear and we would find ourselves presented with a new course of the meal as though it had been produced by a superb sleight-of-hand.

At one time during the dinner, Hugo, the dune poet who lived in a combination shack-tent among the dance halls on the pier, leaned forward and looked deeply into the Sanyassin's eyes.

"You," said Hugo, "have come from the Masters of the Himalayas to comfort and instruct the dunites."

"And you," responded the Sanyassin, "have kissed the Blarney Stone that you may better know how to flatter and bemuse the Master's messengers."

Whiteman, the writer, broke in with, "Oh Hugo, you old faker. You've found your better at last." And then, as writers are wont to do, he launched into an exposition of Hugo's personal life.

He told of how he had found Hugo sleeping on the bare sand just a few hundred feet from the fences of his rich admirers and disciples in Santa Barbara. When Whiteman asked him why he did not let his affluent chelas support him, Hugo frowned, saying, "But I have a reputation to live up to."

Whiteman continued his stories about Hugo, but Hugo had sunk into meditation and apparently did not listen. Neither did the Sanyassin, whose fine sense of tact forbade his showing interest in or even hearing gossip of this sort.

After the banquet, Whiteman took us in his car to the grocer who was delighted with the prospect of having the Sanyassin's clams instead of Dreamwood's paintings. It seemed that, only that morning, a rich Filipino farmer had told the grocer that he would contract for as many as fifty clams a day if the grocer could guarantee regular delivery.

Hill House, where Gavin lived, crowned a low hill with discreet majesty. Gavin met us in the garden and served tomato juice with vodka as we relaxed and talked between brooding Eucalyptus trees.

He fired questions at the Sanyassin with his usual disarming insistence. These questions the Sanyassin answered promptly and politely without revealing a thing and gradually and inconspicuously he turned the conversation from himself to Hill House. What was the mystery of this Eastern house in a Western setting? What had lent this charm of China to the sandy beaches of California?

Gavin loved to talk about his rambling castle, particularly about the eight-walled library built from lumber washed ashore from the wreckage of a Norwegian freighter. And so, for a time, we talked of the library and of the other parts of the house. But after a time, our talk turned to the problem of the time.

While Gavin was a member of the leisure class, his heart was with the simple, uncomplicated life of the dunites. And it had begun to look like the dunes were threatened with extinction.

Land owned by the Santa Barbara Gun Club bordered Mirror Lake on whose shores stood Dreamwood's cabin. Recently, the economic boom had increased the membership of the club so that bullets sometimes sprayed about Dreamwood's cabin and threatened his pet owl and upset his goat. Dead ducks fell on his doorstep. And there was, or so it seemed, nothing which Dreamwood could do because he did not even own the land.

Gavin had tried to help by wielding his considerable influence, but his influence was not enough. It looked as though it would be only a matter of time until Dreamwood was forced out and little more time until the beloved dunes would be the foundations for freeways and hot dog stands and ugly apartment houses.

The Sanyassin listened to Gavin explaining the predicament but he did not seem to share Gavin's sadness.

"But there is no problem," said the Sanyassin, when Gavin paused.

Gavin looked at him angrily. He thought the Sanyassin

was making light of a serious thing. But before Gavin could control his anger enough to speak, the Sanyassin explained, "Squatters' rights," he said. "From looking in Dreamwood's cabin, I know he must have lived there at least twelve years and that's all he needs."

So with Gavin's backing, Dreamwood sued and won, saving his own place and indirectly saving all the dunes. On the day of the verdict, the rabbits and ducks and other small animals reappeared in the greenery about the lake. One baby rabbit found a nest in the grass beneath a painting which Dreamwood had set outside to dry and which he had entitled "All beauty begins at the vanishing point of the seeming self."

Dreamwood's victory made the whole dune feel secure and accepted by society. Nevertheless, his success aroused the ire and envy of a group of aspiring yogis who had always held that Dreamwood's vibrations were not quite as unworldly as they should be. These malcontents held a secret spiritual council to decide on the best course of action.

Finally, it was decided that the simplest means of destroying improper vibrations was by fire. Dreamwood's cabin would have to be burned. But, then, another question intruded. Should Dreamwood be in or out of the cabin when it was set afire? The most effective thing, for the aspirant's purposes should be to include Dreamwood in the purification. This would solve their problem once and for all and would, after all, be doing Dreamwood himself a favor since he would be reborn in a more auspicious incarnation.

But some of the cooler and more practical realized that to burn Dreamwood would very likely bring undesirable complications. Oceano had recently felt that it had become enough of a metropolis to acquire a sheriff, and sheriffs had the habit of interfering with such business as burning undesirable neighbors, even in the dunes. Finally, after much discussion and contemplation, it was decided to burn the cabin while Dreamwood was at the pier picking up his groceries.

The Sanyassin outlined all this to John and me after we found him one morning wetting gunny sacks in the surf. With dripping armloads of burlap, we followed him to Dreamwood's cabin, wondering as we ran how he had come to know things which old dunites like John and me had not had an inkling of.

We reached the cabin and began to fight the fire, which fortunately had not yet really taken hold. As I was pounding at the burning wood with a gunny sack, I suddenly was distracted from the fire by a signal from the Sanyassin.

I turned and saw that one of the arsonists had lifted his axe to cut John down from behind. Almost in reflex, I swung the heavy, wet burlap at his head and it wrapped about his face and he dropped the axe. He struggled with the strangling burlap for a moment and then unwrapped it from about his face. With a sobered eye, he looked at John's seven feet, now facing him, and at the Sanyassin's formidable musculature and then at me, a bundle of fury, and without further argument, turned and fled, followed by the rest of his group.

The three of us returned to the fire, but stopped in a moment when we saw two of the arsonists returning. We faced them, ready for a fight, but their spell had been broken and, in repentance, they had returned to help douse the fire.

I have often mused upon the fact that the Sanyassin, who first saw the axe-wielding arsonist and who was closer to him than I was, did not take the opportunity to subdue him himself. He might have wished to give me that pleasure, seeing my zeal, or he might have wished to remain unencumbered, ready for an attack by the others. But I think probably that it was principle which stopped him. He was a Sanyassin, not a man of violence, even against a violent one.

Two days' hard work by six men, including the two repentant arsonists, restored Dreamwood's cabin to more than its former glory. And the story of the arsonists lived on as a double warning: a warning never to offend the vibratory instincts of the chosen; and above all, never to take the law of Karma into your own hands.

Pat, the escapist, didn't quite get the last point. And he appeared in the dunes at a time when the attempted burning of Dreamwood's cabin was still uncomfortably recent. Pat broke out of any prison with elegance and, seemingly, with little effort, but he could not break away from his superstitions.

I went to visit Pat shortly after he had established himself in a veritable estate, a luxurious combination of two driftwood shacks which I had once occupied. I suppose he chose that particular place because it was as far away from the sheriff's office as possible.

The code of the dunites prescribed that newcomers were entitled to visits from the old-timers, so I arrived at Pat's cabin attired formally in the ragged remains of a woolen bathing suit. As I entered the clearing, I noticed with surprise that one of the cabins lay in ashes. From the inside of the other cabin there came a mumbling voice, sounding as though it chanted incantations.

I listened to the strange sounds for a moment and then knocked. The mumbles ceased, but there was no answer to my knocking. After a moment, I tried again.

A thunderous voice roared, "Who the hell is there?"

Startled, I didn't answer, but just pushed the door open. Pat's face looked out at me and changed from a worried scowl to a smile of relief.

"Oh," he said. "It's only you. Hello. God bless you."

We talked for a while and, eventually, I asked about the burned cabin.

Pat's eyes narrowed. "That blasted shack had an evil spirit in it. So I burned it down."

"I see," I said, a little disturbed.

"And there's others around," he said. "But don't you worry. I can sniff 'em out like skunks. I'll take care of 'em."

With visions of burning cabins dotting the dunes, many of them inhabited, I took my leave as soon as possible and sought out the Sanyassin.

He calmly heard me out and then said, "I believe we shall introduce Pat to John."

His answer disappointed me. I had expected him to formulate a resourceful scheme for ousting the madman from the dunes or a plan for reforming him. Instead, he proposed widening his circle of acquaintances.

We went along with John to Pat's cabin. I noted an ominous touch to the tall man's long strides as we crossed the sand, but he calmly greeted Pat, looking at him with friendship. And then his eyes fell on the pile of unwashed dishes and pots and pans in the cabin.

"I shall help you wash these," said John. "We like for the dune cabins to be tidy."

Thereafter, John arrived at Pat's shack at six o'clock every morning and helped him tidy up the inside and worked with him in keeping weeds and snakes out of his well. In a few days, the cabin, inside and out, was spick and span. Finally, I began to understand.

Within a week, Pat left the dunes leaving no trace. Another of the Sanyassin's strange methods.

In the case of Whiteman versus the dunites, the Sanyassin surprised us all by playing a more active role than ever before: he wrote a poem.

Whiteman had been writing books about economics, always covering his real beliefs under a safe gloss of sarcasm. This was becoming to him for he was a visitor in life's garden, not a toiler or any other kind of participant. Similarly, he was a frequent visitor, but never a dunite.

So when he ventured into fiction and wrote a book about the dunes, it had the same distant, overbearing, sarcastic flavor. He could not even keep to the present, but made frequent forays into past dune lore and the legends of some early squatter who had lived in the dunes while waiting for ancient Lemuria to rise up out of the Pacific Ocean. These long-ago residents seem to have spent most of their time on the beach, breathing in chorus and sighing, "Lemuria" into the west. To their astonished disappointment, Lemuria did not appear, but they remained sure that it eventually would.

At last, one of them had a vision. The faithful must prepare themselves by a strict diet, eating only "that which hath no face". The vision aroused a controversy. Clams, which were then, as now, amply available, were the staple food. But did the clams have faces?

Whiteman took his novel's theme from this rather ridiculous tale and called his book, *The Face of the Clam.* But while writing about the actions of past residents, his love for the present overtook him and he switched carelessly to Dreamwood, Hugo, and the rest of us, making it seem as if we, too, were breathlessly looking for Lemuria.

To such as John and the Sanyassin and me, the thing did not matter. We cared little about what a book by a writer such as Whiteman might do to our reputations. But there were others who had high and strangely vulnerable opinions of themselves and they threatened to bar the "traitor-author" from the dunes forever, by force, if necessary.

The Sanyassin, who evidently could not stand unresolved quarrels, came to the rescue with his poem:

As time and space come bending back

To catch this ancient talk,

And bring it round to driftwood shack,

In cool, green, shady vale,

We bearded guardians of truth,

On hearing it, may think

Our past and present lost, forsooth,

In space-time's lacy link.

But babbling spirits, 'twixt the coves,

Are laughing with delight.

And great white souls in shapes of doves

Are chortling in their might:

"Tis Whiteman, silent watcher, out riding in the night.

A-towering, a-tearing, a-goggling and a-goring,

A-guffawing, a-gossiping, awaking dark and bright ones,

A-chasing off too light ones, a-calling all the right ones,

Announcing score of fight.

'Tis Whiteman in the night!"

The poem, simple as it was, seemed to put Whiteman in his proper place. Then, with peace apparently once more firmly established in the dunes, I went off to war.

During the turbulent and dangerous time which followed, I found my mind turning often to the peace and solitude and beauty of the dunes. It was good to carry with me a memory of paradise which really existed somewhere on this very planet which was torn with the grim realities of World War.

The dunes were a place where time stood still. A place with little official interference or insolence. A place which did not confine one within four walls except at night, and not always then. A place which did not imprison our bodies and souls in steel or concrete monsters, directly, as the mean and simple do, or subtly, by the persuasion of custom and alleged economy, as the civilized do.

And gradually, as the War wore on, my mind kept coming back more and more often to the Sanyassin and his role in the dunes. Why was this strange and likeable man so determined to maintain the status quo of the dunes?

A humorous answer occurred to me: it was to keep

his clams circulating – from him, through and for the benefit of Dreamwood, to the grocer, and then to the rich Filipino farmer. Clams. Clams! This was ridiculous. But my mind kept returning to the clams. Sometimes I dreamed about the faces of the clams.

But finally, the War was finished and I was free to return to the dunes. I invited a friend and fellow from Army Intelligence, Rene, and the both of us hurried across the Atlantic and across the country to the dunes. Never, in my thoughts during the years I was away, had I considered the possibility of change. I had gone on assuming that the same people would still be there when I returned, in the same setting. Only as we were leaving Oceano and beginning the walk across the dunes, did the fear and the realization of the possibility of change strike me.

But the same cranes and storks were still selecting their menus with majestic disdain from the shallow creek which still wandered coolly among the tall reeds and pussy willows between banks covered with bursts of brightly-colored flowers. A shimmering, subtropic haze hung overhead and beyond the expanse of yellow sand was the sapphire-blue ocean.

This was my return. I looked aside at Rene. The beauty was not all in my own eyes. There was an urgency about him and, when we turned south along the beach, he rushed along the wet sand, past the serenely-staring pelicans. Then, when we turned back inland, his long legs outran me completely. He turned and gave me a grateful look from the point where the greenery sprang up from the sand and then he hurried on, heading right for Dreamwood's cabin as if he had known this path all his life.

Dreamwood was not at home, but before he left, he had put his paintings out to take the sun and I found Rene admiring them as I came panting up.

"These are fabulous," he said. "But, of course, the titles must be changed."

"Of course," I said, looking once more at the crimson splotch entitled, "All beauty begins at the vanishing point of the seeming-self," and remembering finding the bunny hiding beneath it.

"The man's a great artist, except with words," said Rene. "It's our duty as officers and gentlemen to help him."

We set about writing out new titles on little bits of paper which we fastened with pins above the old so that our changes were not irreversible. The crimson blotch we called, "Atom bombs play baseball." A monumental canvas featuring dark, amorphous bodies entangled in a bitter struggle was titled by Dreamwood, "Astral studies from the Atman plane." We retitled it, "The Battle of the Bulges."

Rene sudden froze and stared at the edge of the clearing. There, not fifty feet away, sat the Sanyassin. He looked like a man just waking from a deep sleep. He smiled lightly at me and then looked at Rene with a quiet, measured gaze which seemed to encompass everything. Rene looked back, like a man who is finally face to face with that which he has been seeking, or chasing.

The appearance of the Sanyassin in that spot amazed me. I could not believe that he could have approached and sat down without our seeing him. And it was equally unbelievable that he could have been there all the time.

It was as though he had simply materialized in that spot.

Finally, I was able to speak. "Where is Dreamwood?" I asked.

"I am afraid he has been detained in town," answered the Sanyassin. At that moment, I noticed how pale he was and how deeply thoughtful.

"Detained," I said, fearing the connotations of the word. "You can't mean by the sheriff."

"Yes," he answered. "So I have heard." His voice was heavy and tired.

"But that's ridiculous," I said.

"Yes," said the Sanyassin softly. "Ridiculous."

"We must get him out."

The Sanyassin looked at me gratefully with tired, hurt eyes. "I had hoped that you would."

Rene and I set out for Oceano immediately. The Sanyassin did not follow.

We found Dreamwood sitting in a cell in the town jail, deep in meditation. He seemed amost to resent our intrusion, but he bowed graciously to Rene.

"What's going on, Dreamwood?" I asked him.

He shrugged and smiled as if the thing did not really concern him. "Ask the sheriff," he said.

We did. The sheriff frowned and said, "Dreamwood is being held on a very serious charge. He seemed sorry to have to give us the news. He seems to be involved in dope smuggling," he finally said.

I was amazed and furious. "You can't be serious!"

"It's true," said the sheriff apologetically.

"But you can't believe that Dreamwood is guilty of that."

The sheriff shook his head. "Frankly, no. But he's our only possible suspect and he won't even try to defend himself."

"What is the connection?" I asked.

"The clams," said the sheriff. "The clams that are left on the pier in exchange for his groceries."

Somehow, I had expected this very answer, but my world collapsed and, for a moment, I could not speak. My faithful, always kind, courteous friend, the Sanyassin! I saw him in my mind, suddenly appearing at the edge of the clearing near Dreamwood's cabin, sending us after Dreamwood, but not coming with us.

"There's only one answer," I said to the sheriff. "Let Dreamwood go and we will watch all his movements. My friend Rene is one of the most famous Army Intelligence officers. He will help me. Release Dreamwood in our custody and we'll soon find the answers."

Dreamwood came out of his cell as if nothing had happened and this mood continued all the way to his cabin. Rene and I followed along behind him, not disturbing him.

When we reached his cabin, his meditation did not prevent him from seeing the new names we had put on his paintings. He looked at them, one by one, and then fixed Rene with a look so fixed and angry that it made my stomach feel hollow. Rene answered him with a grin which just intensified the look on Dreamwood's face.

"Don't be angry," I said to Dreamwood. "It was all in fun. They can be taken off."

I knelt and pulled off a couple of the scraps of paper. Dreamwood looked at me with a look which was almost friendly and then turned his fixed, hurt look back on Rene. He was not at all concerned with being suspected of dope smuggling, but he was terribly hurt because we had tampered with the names of his paintings.

With a shrug, I left them to settle their differences and hurried to the point on the beach where I had first seen the Sanyassin so long ago. He was there, methodically donning his skindiving gear which I had not seen since his first day in the dunes.

"I'm glad you came," he said easily.

"Why did you do it?"

He smiled and it seemed to me to be the warmest, kindest smile I had ever seen. "*Why* is a tiger with a thousand tails! You cut off one of them and three new ones appear to take its place. In other words, my friend, we are drawn into our thought patterns and activities by forces which we do not know. We may give a thousand reasons for our actions, but chances are, none of them is correct."

"High school children buy those powders," I said, becoming outraged with his lack of concern. "They may become ruined for life. It could be your son or daughter."

Now the Sanyassin looked very serious. "Tragedy comes when weakness meets temptation. But the real tragedy is the weakness. Temptation will always be at hand."

"You can't be saying that you went into this dirty business to provide temptation to test, and possibly strengthen, the weak?"

He smiled. "No. Not exactly. Have you ever, by chance, read about the white settlers, who, some years ago, forced China into an opium trade which nearly wrecked the country?"

"And now you're taking revenge?" I asked, unbelievingly. "But you're not Chinese."

"I am not taking revenge and I am not defending myself. There is nothing to defend." He smiled. "But you may contemplate the elaborate pattern of fate. Our forefathers nearly wrecked China by enforcing a criminal opium trade. Today China is taking a mild sort of revenge. She is not wrecking the descendants of her tormentors. The dope trade has hardly any effect on the American or any other nation. It wrecks only a few weaklings who would be destroyed by something, sooner or later. But the net effect is to stir up the West and make its people think and reflect and, perhaps, make amends."

The Sanyassin was gathering up the last of his gear. Out of the corner of my eye, I saw two shapes come running over the top of a dune. The Sanyassin did not look their way, but a smile played lightly on his lips.

"I don't want an incident," he said. "So I shall leave you now. Tell the sheriff whatever you wish and keep loveable Dreamwood out of trouble." He smiled one last time. "I shall remember you a long, long time," he said, and stepped leisurely into the edge of the ocean.

When John and Rene reached the beach, the Sanyassin was far enough out that he was able to dive gracefully into a wave and disappear. They both, without hesitation, plunged into the ocean after him and I woke, as if from a dream, and followed them.

I was a good swimmer and not out of breath from running as were John and Rene and I passed them and was very close to the Sanyassin when he surfaced. He smiled and waved to me.

"You are my kind of people," he called, his voice carrying above the roar of the surf. "The others live by principle, and that is a sterling quality, but you, you live by wisdom." And then he dove and I never saw him again.

Boats put out to sea in search for the Sanyassin but they found no trace. Wild stories circulated that they had heard a humming noise which they identified as being the engines of a submarine. And there were several who claimed that they had seen a man rise out of the sea and soar into the sky, trailing luminescence behind him like the tail of a comet.

That night, I walked aimlessly along the Pacific through heavy fog, lost in thought. Finally, the howls of coyotes roused my consciousness and I found that I had lost my way. For a long time, I wandered among the dunes, growing more unsure of my location all the time. The howls of the coyotes pursued me. These cowardly small animals will sometimes attack a man in the fog if there are enough of them. And it is very dangerous to stop and sit or lie down to rest. But at last, I was exhausted and I did not care about the coyotes. My greatest friend had, perhaps, betrayed my faith. It had left a sore emptiness inside me. I stopped, feeling unable to take another step, and began to lower myself to the sand.

And then, suddenly, something soft swept against my forehead. I was startled wide awake and tried to see something in the foggy darkness. It came again, bumping softly, but deliberately, against my forehead. This time I made out a gray shape in the air. A bird.

I walked in the direction from which it came. Many times, as I walked along, it gently buffeted my hair and forehead, as if to make sure that I would follow. At last, I saw lights and found myself at the door of Dreamwood's cabin. As I was about to knock, I saw the bird appear out of the fog and take its usual perch. It was Dreamwood's owl. It settled softly and embraced me with its all-knowing eyes – the eyes of the Sanyassin.

The Tale of Trailanga

It was Fitzgerald who prompted the story of Trailanga. He was sitting behind his desk, touching a Tibetan mask plucked from the litter on his desk, when he mentioned that he had, at some time, heard someone speak of the *Legend of Trailanga*. He wondered if I knew the story.

Trailanga is, today, only a legend, a Buddha-bellied statue and, for a very few fortunate ones, an actual memory.

Tourists find that there are very many things in India which they are forbidden to photograph and it is always amusing to watch them approach the Trailanga Shrine. They approach the impressive statue in the front of the shrine and surreptitiously raise their cameras. Suddenly, they feel a gentle tap on the shoulder and turn to confront the all-seeing Sadhu who stands watch over the shrine. The tourist feels that all is up. But the Sadhu steps forward and lifts the cloth which covers the huge pot-belly of the statue and invites the tourist to take his photograph of the statue with the belly exposed so that it may shine forth with proper glory from the picture. There seems to be a feeling in India that the more of God's space you occupy, the greater your honor.

It was as a result of bathing in the Ganges that I came to be told of Trailanga by one of his disciples. As every visitor to India knows, bathing in the Ganges forgives your sins and those of your progeny for three generations. I was in India and my family was with me when this story took place.

I am not sure that I am entirely convinced of the efficacy of bathing in the Ganges, but I decided that, after all, it would not hurt anything and it might help. So I proceeded with my family to a convenient place where the Ganges roars out of the Himalayas and is not yet contaminated by too many sins or other impurities, spiritual or physical.

If someone doubts that a mere dip in the sacred Ganges will forgive his trespasses, India's ancient civilization has the answer even for him. If he is the worldly type who doubts the word "sin", or that it needs to be forgiven, he is told with an indulgent smile that this custom arose so that the people would bathe and keep themselves clean. After all, is it not true that a dip in the Ganges will forgive the sin of uncleanliness?

But if the doubter is of serious thought who well realizes that there is sin and virtue, folly and wisdom, but that wisdom and virtue can hardly be had for the moderate price of a bathe in a river, then these wise ones are taken into the sanctum of the initiates and told that the Ganges is only a symbol like the Jamuna for the Vaishnavas and the Jordan for the Christians.

These rivers are symbols of creative forces, heard by some as sounds, issuing like a stream or river, from unknown higher regions. An earnest seeker may feel it or hear it. It is the answer of God to one with steadfast concentration. And the sins of him who can hear or feel it and who can remain with it and fathom its depth are wiped out, as are those of his friends and his children and his children's children. He has come far on the way home to his Creator, in Whom there is no sin.

For the purpose of conveniently entering the holy waters, wide marble steps have been built down into the river. The bathers climb down the steps into the water and bathe themselves and each other with great ease.

On the day when my wife and I went to the river, a good crowd thronged the steps. My wife purchased a pail of water from the river with which to perform her symbolic bathing, but I was determined to do the job thoroughly.

From the top of the marble steps, I surveyed the situation. It took off the robe I wore and was suddenly struck with the feeling that the brief red trunks I wore were improper. I was embarrassed at the thought of waiting for the crowd, so I disregarded the swiftness of the water and launched myself in a long dive and struck the water, chillingly cold from having run down from the melting snow in the mountains, at a good distance from the bank in the teeth of the frothing current.

For a short time I struggled to swim back toward the bank, but made no headway and felt my strength ebbing. Then, suddenly, an exhilaration struck me and my strength was renewed and, with strong, sure strokes I defeated the current and emerged from the cold water in the midst of the crowd on the steps. The crowd greeted me with an ovation, but looking up, I saw three elder Yogis watching me sternly from the top of the steps.

Climbing the steps quickly, I hurriedly donned my

robe and approached the three, expecting censure. Could my brief trunks have offended their sense of propriety?

"No," answered the oldest of the three. "Our stern looks were merely because we were concentrating upon you against the strength of the current."

I was struck silent in astonishment. So that was the reason for my surge of strength.

"About your attire," said the youngest, smiling, "my elder brother could tell you about Trailanga – he actually saw him – and that would put you at your ease."

The oldest of them nodded solemnly, his white beard caressing his chest. "Trailanga," he said, "was the greatest among us. He carried his three hundred pounds with grace and zest. He came down out of the wilds of the Himalayas and, even in these civilized surroundings, could never remember to put on any clothes, not even the briefest of briefs. He was the incarnation of innocence. We knew this and everyone in this place, even the police, knew it and we all respected him deeply and so all went well."

The old Yogi paused and looked out over the Ganges, as if counting his memories, and then continued.:

But then Trailanga was struck with a strong urge to visit Bengal. We tried to persuade him not to go, knowing the limited understanding and humor of the Bengali police. But Trailanga put off our protestations, saying that Bengali souls were clamoring for his presence.

He was arrested, as we had foreseen, by the austere Bengali police. They locked him in a cell hardly large enough for him to squeeze into despite the fact that weeping and shamed men and women almost mobbed the police. Everyone was upset except Trailanga. He smiled serenely as he was locked away.

The policeman put a padlock on the door of the cell and then went out to keep watch on the milling crowd. Suddenly, the yelling of the mob stopped and they looked up in stunned surprise and then began to clap and cheer. The bewildered policemen looked up on the roof and saw Trailanga happily sunning himself in all three hundred pounds of his uncovered glory.

The unappreciative policemen went to the roof and hauled the huge Yogi down. He did not seem to mind at all and offered no resistance, but smiled good-naturedly, as they put him back into the cell. This time, in addition to the padlock, they posted two armed guards at the cell door.

The policeman again came out to the front of the jail and found the crowd watching the roof and applauding more enthusiastically than before. Again the policemen found Trailanga bathing his huge body in the good Bengali sun.

"Do you mean Trailanga hypnotized the crowd into believing he was sitting on the roof?" I asked.

The old man slowly shook his head. "A real Yogi never hypnotizes anybody. Trailanga was on the roof. The policemen went to his cell. He was not there."

I seemed to be only a shade from a deep and mystic secret. "How do you explain it?" I asked, hopefully. "How could such a thing happen?"

"How does it happen that a dropped stone falls?" he asked. "How did it happen that you were not swept downstream and drowned?"

For a time, the old man was lost in thought and then he continued.

Finally, the policemen summoned their chief who surveyed the situation and then politely approached Trailanga. "Please, good sir," said the chief with great deference, "might I prevail upon you to do your sunbathing elsewhere?"

"Why, certainly," answered Trailanga, all in smiles. "Whatever you wish. And please forgive me. I was under the impression your men wished me to stay."

After having blessed the crowd, Trailanga walked down to the Ganges. There, he seated himself upon the surface of the river and floated gently downstream, his formidable posterior barely touching the water.

"Now when we saw you diving into the river," said the old Yogi, "we were not quite sure if we had a Yogi before us who was about to perform like Trailanga or if the strong current might sweep you to a premature crossing of the River of Death. So we concentrated or, as you say in your country, we prayed for your safety."

I thanked him and admitted that I was not at all sure that I could reproduce Trailanga's feats, but that I would work toward it. I asked him if he, who had known Trailanga and who was an initiate, would be an example and an encouragement to me by giving me a demonstration.

There was a father's tender look in the old Yogi's eyes as he gently shook his head. "Trailanga had come far in mastering his mind and his body, but not so far in gauging the effects of his actions on others. If I were to repeat his feats and stir you to try to emulate me and, if you were then to fail, frustration and weakened faith in yourself would be your reward. What you want to do, you, yourself must do. None other can do it for you."

"But how can I?"

"Any man can do anything he wants to do," said the old Yogi, "if he really wants to do it. And if he does not set impossible conditions."

"What sort of impossible conditions?"

"Such as demanding to be able to do it right now, without preparation. There must be no limit to the effort of time which he is willing to spend," said the Yogi solemnly.

"Will you help me – teach me?"

"On those conditions, yes," he answered. "But do not be surprised if, in mid-course, when your wisdom has grown, you find that there is a more worthwhile goal for you to pursue."

With that, the three of them politely took their leave.

The Tale of Fu Kieng

The trip to the Kumbha Mela at last began. After the days of preparation, the swiftness of the jet-engined plane appeared anticlimactic as it seemed that we were picked up and then immediately set down halfway around the world. But weather delayed us and we missed our flight out of Hong Kong and were forced, not too much against our half-conscious wish, to stay over a day.

My anticipation of coming events had brought to mind a night in Badrinath, under the spell of a being somewhat similar to the one I hoped we would meet at this time. My three companions flattered me by staying on in the hotel to listen to my report, rather than taking the grand tour of Kowloon and the New Territories.

The hair fell softly over wide shoulders and a very straight back. Above that poised head, the twin peaks of Badrinath, on the Tibetan Border, were hazily outlined against the first grey of dawn. I could not see his eyes in the half-dark, but they were still clearly imprinted upon my retina since the day before – deep pools of understanding, brimming with sympathy.

How could any harm come to such a being at such a place? My imagination must have played pranks with me. Besides, Fu Kieng was snoring gently in his bunk. No need for my imposed vigil!

I was about to return to the whitewashed dormitory with its smell of antiseptics when I saw the gleam. In two bounds I was upon the attacker. As we went down I saw his sleek features. It was Raj. I had appraised his strength many times during our trip. With my two hands I gripped his one hand holding the knife. But it was slipping. How long could I hold out?

To this nagging doubt was added concern about the guards. If they were attracted by our struggle, would I be able to convince them that I, a foreigner, was protecting their saint from murder by one of their own countrymen? Or would they simply assume that the foreigner was to blame and summarily hack me down?

Intertwined with these unhappy thoughts, came a keen, sharp memory of all that had gone on along the pilgrim road. I saw Fu Kieng's frightened face before me once again as he asked Shri Swayumbi if the saint had lions or tigers to protect him. I remembered Shri Swayumbi's indulgent smile as he assured him that the Badrinath saint was a man of God, not of tigers. And I remembered being puzzled at Fu Kieng's obvious relief.

Why was Fu Kieng so concerned about who or what protected the saint? Why did he go to Badrinath at all? It was not like a Chinese man to be interested in Indian saints and it certainly was not characteristic of Fu Kieng.

The first time I had noticed Fu Kieng was at Rishikesh. We were a busload of pilgrims going to see the Saint of Badrinath and our bus had made a stop in this picturesque place. Immediately after we came to a stop, a surprisingly clean and well-groomed hand was thrust in through the brass railing of the first-class compartments and, before the rest of us realized that the hand belonged to a government agent, a Chinese man had surrendered his immunization certificate and then the rest of us followed suit. That had been my first glimpse of Fu Kieng.

I was intrigued by him. It seemed odd that a Chinese man should be on such a pilgrimage. And it was also unusual that he was accompanied by an Indian man, the powerful Raj.

His knife hand was almost loose now. In a matter of seconds, he would have the knife free and would stab me with it. Then he would tell the guards that he had heroically saved the venerable saint from the vicious attack of a foreign evildoer.

Above us, on the boulder, the blessed saint was looking mildly into the coming dawn, seemingly unaware that a struggle to the death was going on at his feet on his behalf.

Raj twisted his head and bit fiercely at my right hand. The pain was unbearable and I was about to let go and then I realized that Raj would not just kill me and say that he had saved the life of the saint. No. He would kill me and then kill the saint and say that he had caught me fleeing after I had killed the saint and then performed an execution. The injustice struck me and I tightened my grip and ignored the pain.

After the holy ones of the Shivanand Ashram in Rishikesh had blessed us all, and after the blowing of horns and a great deal of shouting, our caravan of buses moved on. Fu Kieng looked out through the brass grill which enclosed the first-class compartment and down into the abyss thousands of feet below, on the edge of which our bus driver careened unconcernedly. Fu Kieng's face turned green. His companion, Raj, looked disgusted.

When we stopped at a roadside inn, Fu Kieng's color returned to normal. At dinner, he and his companion took a table next to mine and we nodded courteously. Later, we were given a room to share, but we were all tired and did not make much conversation even though I was very interested in finding out just what attraction an Indian saint had for Fu Kieng. Raj, I rather ignored. He seemed a pleasant enough young man, but there was no mystery about him.

Raj! Yes. He was the one I should have watched. He was the one with the knife which was surely slipping free to be plunged into my flesh while the intended victim, the saint, sat blandly by, seeming to know nothing of what transpired at his feet. But then, on the heels of my thought of his disdain, it seemed as though I saw a flash of fire in the peaceful eyes of the saint. But then, there was nothing. I believed I had imagined it.

My thoughts escaped from my doom back to the pilgrimage. The most difficult thing about a pilgrimage in India is that you cannot buy one ticket for a long bus trip, but must queue up again and again to buy tickets for the next leg of the journey. And every queue seems to be composed of a thousand whirling dervishes and yourself.

Fu Kieng, I was glad to see, was as helpless as myself in the ticket queue. We were buffeted together by the crowd and he said, shouting above the noise, "Are you sure we're getting anywhere?"

"I'm sure we're not," I answered.

But suddenly a six and a half foot tall Indian wearing a well-trimmed beard approached the queue. For a moment he looked down at Fu Kieng and myself and then looked over the mass of people about us. "Preposterous!" he said. Then he waded through the crowd, into the office of the bus line.

"Our foreign guest over there," I heard him say, "the Chinese and the American..."

"You're American," exclaimed Fu Kieng, looking at me with sudden distaste.

I ignored him for the moment and listened to the huge Indian. "The queue has constantly by passed those two," he said, "simply because they are polite – more polite than we are. Have we a right to prevent them from reaching their pilgrim's destination for that reason?"

In a moment, Fu Kieng and I were handed tickets while our gallant sponsor went back to his place in the queue, true to the faith of all good yogis that one should act for the sake of the just cause, but not for personal gain.

Fu Kieng and I boarded the bus, meeting Raj, who had not had our troubles. Very soon, we were moving again. Our bearded Indian friend, diverting our attention from the abyss below, pointed toward the peaks ahead, saying, "Millions of souls, for thousands of years, have thrust their devotions upon those giants and, lo, now they return this power, this blessing, a thousandfold. Do you not feel it?"

Fu Kieng did not feel it. He did not even listen. He turned angrily toward me. "You Americans," he said. "You hate all us Chinese, don't you?"

"Why no," I said. "We admire you with a touch of frenzy. Don't we know that your civilization is many centuries older than ours?"

He was taken aback. "You do?" he said, amazed. "Could you ever think of ... helping Chinese?"

"Of course," I answered with sincerity. "I would consider it an honor."

Then, as I seemed close to gaining the confidence of this man and satisfying my curiosity, he became silent and uncommunicative, seeming frightened. Ignoring me, he listened enthusiastically to the huge, bearded Indian's talk about the mountains.

It would not be long now. The point of the knife hypnotized me as it slowly moved toward my throat. There was no fright in my mind. Death seemed so certain and so near that there was no place for fear. I escaped into more memories of the pilgrimage.

On the last leg of the trip, from Bela Kushi to Joshimath, there was a reassuring sound which kept us from worrying about the abyss into which the insouciant bus driver seemed certain to drop us. Someone was snoring. If someone felt that tranquil about the trip, what was there to worry about? We were doubly reassured when investigation showed us that the calm snores belonged to the venerable chief police official of the district.

But his wife was not reassured. "Bahadur," she called. "Bahadur!" She shoved at his arm. "Wake up."

With sputtering groans, the sleepy policeman came to. He looked around disappointedly.

"Bahadur," said his wife. "Don't you see that we are in mortal danger? How can you nap like this?"

Bahadur rubbed his eyes and looked out at the abyss and quickly withdrew his glance.

"Mortal danger?" He said. "Well, if so, why didn't you let me sleep? What better than to sleep painlessly into the glorious death of the Himalayas?"

"What is so glorious about it?" asked a fellow passenger.

Bahadur rose to the question. "For one thing," he said with great dignity, "if you die while on pilgrimage, you are reborn as a little child in the Himalayas and you will become the chela of a rishi."

"Have you ever met a real rishi?" I inquired.

"Oh, no," said Bahadur, holding up his hands. "I would be afraid."

His wife shot a sharp glance at him.

"My dear," he said to her, "I would be afraid – for you. If I ever met such a one, I would forget my duties, my family, everything, and join his flock of chelas."

"Hmmpf," interrupted the wife. "Do you think the great ones need chelas who go to sleep when danger threatens?"

The hand which held the knife was slipping out of my grasp. The tragic end was near. Without hope, I cast what I thought would be my last glance at the serene saint for whom I was now to die, without glory. As before, he was gazing serenely ahead without the slightest apparent knowledge of my sacrifice.

But at the last possible instant, fire flashed from his eyes into mine. I did not see him move, but he was gripping Raj's wrist with such sudden strength that the knife flipped out of his hand and flew off into the dense underbrush. Raj stared in helpless amazement into the fire of the saint's eyes.

Had the venerable rishi waked from his meditations just in time to act? Or had he seen what was going on all the time and just not bothered to interfere until the last fraction of a second?

For a moment, I was furious at the thought that he might knowingly have let me struggle almost to my death before acting. But then I saw the pettiness of my thoughts in the face of the fact that, just an instant before, that venerable yogi had saved my life.

Finally, now, the guards came running. How could I face them? What could I say?

Even while I tried to think of what to say, a voice, clear and sweet as the morning sounded. "Our foreign guest has saved my life," said the saint, "As to the misguided soul who attacked me, let him leave in peace with his accomplice. They knew not what they did."

A large crowd had gathered and, among the faces, I saw Fu Kieng. I was about to speak to him when the saint's voice came again.

"Fu Kieng! You came to slay an old man in Badrinath – not with your own hands, but with the hand of your willing tool – so that you could then pretend to be the defender of the faith and summon your Chinese soldiers here to protect my bereaved people. But you have failed. Now go back with Raj, to the people who sent you. And tell them about the old man in Badrinath and his friends from far and near."

Communication Without Words

At last. In a rickety taxi whose body was the most international thing I had ever seen, having been repaired over its many years with bits and pieces of almost every sort of vehicle ever built anywhere, the three men of science and I were on the last leg of our journey to Allahabad, the holy city, the site of the Kumbha Mela.

We had just come through a village where we had seen a gathering of brown-skinned children and serene adults in a setting which had not changed in the last five thousand years, when Dr. Jacques Miel spoke.

"These people," he said. "I know that they would accept it if we stopped here and told them that the four of us could communicate without words. Through simplicity and unsophisticated faith, they would accept our statements at face value. But what of people in the United States or Europe? What would they say? I don't mean what would the newspapers say. Newsprint lends itself to automatic cynicism. But, what would the people say?"

"It's an interesting question," I answered. "It happens to be one which I have investigated to some extent:

'To a mind at peace, other minds become open books', said the Ancients.

Today the universities on three continents are testing the truth of this dream in the midst of a world which is anything but at peace. At least two nations are trying to throw light on it through government projects.

But these projects are not held up frankly before the public eye, for what would the taxpayer say to this use of his money? For the price of a small ulcer, a man may become a millionaire so why should he pay for peace and the slight chance of a peek into his neighbor's thoughts? If the project were successful, the wishful thinker would see his castles tumble; the pessimist would see his cherished darkness brightened; and the prober would see his suspicions exchanged for something no more exciting than truth.

Once when I traveled leisurely across the United States, I made a sort of game of asking random persons the question of what they thought of either the feasibility or the virtue of mind-to-mind communication.

Vasily – engineer, late (and happily so) of Russia: I have my doubts about it. So far, even behind the Iron Curtain, they have one thing they can call their own – their thoughts. If even thoughts are open for inspection, what is left? But then, again, if all minds knew the thoughts of all other minds, how could there be any more secret arrests, or crimes or wars? I think totalitarian governments would crumble. Even the governments of the free world would be more careful in their ways.

Rockwood – hermit, shore of Lake Okeechobee: I've tried all my life and failed. I thought a life alone would help me get a real hold on my mind and heart. But I think I was wrong. But now I think that a man living close to other people may do better. Anyway, I know some who can communicate. When it does become a recognized thing, we'll know what others are planning for or against us and be prepared. We'll know our own minds better, too. I think most of our misfortunes come from not really knowing ourselves.

John – sailor, of Los Angeles: On a date, it'd be great. If I knew what a girl was thinking…

Robert – St. Paul newsboy: Gee, it's in the papers all the time. They got scientists and everything working on it. You can't fight it. It's coming.

Fred – Glacier Bay, Alaska, fisherman: I don't know. I never worried about it. If they make it so I can tell right where the fish are, it's okay, I guess.

Chuck – San Francisco, shoe-shine boy: Well, like the guy that just walks off without paying. If I could read the deadbeats like him, great.

Slick – Greybull, Wyoming, ranch hand: you mean mind-reading? Well, it sounds to me like it's something else silly from England. Like that skinny, funny-looking model.

Oklahoma college president: It would certainly help in a football game.

Burt – roustabout from Giddings, Texas: I think it's a good thing. My wife already has it. She always knows when somebody's gonna get hurt on the rig.

Mabel Maleska – Oneonta, New York: You've got to be kidding. No? Well, okay. Bob's my boyfriend and he and I read each other's minds already, with no trouble at all. At least, I read his.

Musician – Boston: What a drab, drab world.

Statesman – Virginia: I can humbly claim some personal knowledge of this matter. The scope it offers for national and international progress is beyond imagination.

Enough of the polling. It was interesting and amusing. But to be more serious, there is an interesting question: Are we looking for a new art or are we just attempting to recover an old one? Most of the universities are working under an assumption based on the first part of the question.

However, most of those who have achieved meaningful communication with other minds do not always know why, but they tend to the second part of the question. They talk of a long-past era when religion was not necessary because the soul, without learning, knew.

But then, the bulk of humanity submerged, like divers, to investigate the dark waters far below. Most of them did not ever again look toward the surface, and those who did saw but a flicker and, later, not even that. So religion was born – a search for far horizons.

Now we have to relearn, through painstaking investigation, the things which have been tucked away for so long, in what some present scientists call 'the subconscious,' a common reservoir of the ages, which other scientists split into 'unconscious' and 'preconscious.' Inaccurate terms, all, covering too much ground, but these are the only words formal science knows.

Some persons are so eager to remove the barrier of the conscious mind that they use drugs. Not all drug users understand what the drug does and not all of them are motivated by a solemn will to remove a barrier. Nevertheless, even alcohol is taken by many to overcome sorrows, awkwardness or to remove the barrier between one's own and other minds. Opium and heroin are often taken for the same reason, at least at first, and for the apparent happiness which comes with forgetting nagging thoughts. Other drugs have a more specific effect in opening other channels to other minds, but all such methods are limited and lead to distortions, never to mastery.

Safe removal of the barrier is achieved by increasingly identifying your aims and objectives, your very life, with those of the Creator. What are the aims and objectives of the Creator? Everyone knows in his heart: growth, be it of trees or animals or men; evolution of mind and heart until great inventions and heroic sacrifices result.

In all known civilizations, as far back as oral or written records go, and possibly before, there were persons of certain schools or orders who repeated, with every breath they took, 'This is not my body. It is the Temple of God,' and 'These thoughts are not mine. They are the Thoughts of God,' and 'This is not my heart. It is the Shrine of God.'

Some modern scholars call it 'self-hypnosis.' But a more correct term would be 'self-control.' Most people today pay no attention to the junk flowing by and into their minds and emotions. In spite of our schools and universities, we allow our minds to become garbage cans. To counter this runaway policy and control the influx, is not hypnosis only for control?

The result of such control is a gradual change of mind and emotions, a general maturing so that thoughts and feelings more and more reflect noble, creative patterns. In a humble way, such a person becomes identified with the Creator and partakes, to some extent, in His vision and power, in His insight into the minds and hearts of other persons.

In this game, humility is the secret password and also the sign of the true. There is not room for two separate persons in one mind or, even more so, in one heart. So the seeker tries to erase completely his own self and his own wishes and ideas to make room for the Creator, whom many call 'The Only Being'.

And here, a question arises. Is it really possible for a human being to raise himself up into a knowing, almost divine status in this manner? If it is, then it would seem the greatest quest. If it is not, it still remains important to purify mind and heart by controlling the influx. No one can know without trying. And it would seem a worthwhile try. All religious traditions insist that it can be done, that it is the law of life and the purpose of man and the universe. A few persons have had the privilege of meeting someone who seemed to them to have succeeded.

The pinnacle of modern Western Civilization is the scholar, the scientist who, after years of patient study, may find a piece of truth. To expand this fragment and fit it into the larger pattern, he must humble himself to the state of the mystic, with no thought of self and not the slightest ambition. Then he may reach the wider goal, when he least suspects it and after all notion of self has passed.

Therefore, when a man says, I can read your thoughts, he cannot. No one can read another's thoughts. No one has that right or that power. But when a man loses himself and lives in the eternal, he lives in all, loves all and knows the thoughts of another as he once knew his own. For now. For a moment, he truly is that other person. As soon as he ceased to be that other person, he can no longer know his thoughts.

Very few who set out to reach this state ever fully succeed. But they always benefit by just having undertaken the journey. They gain in health, wisdom, clarity of mind and purity of feelings. No harm can come from setting out on this path, so we may safely attempt to explore it.

Modern medical science often refers to 'psychosomatic' cases, meaning physical conditions brought about by psychological factors, or vice-versa, thoughts and feelings being caused by physical factors. But ages ago, dervishes ate crushed glass or poisonous insects without the slightest discomfort, simply through mental and emotional control of their bodily functions. At this present time, there are two women in India who have eaten nothing for many years and yet are in excellent health. They are currently under close observation by Indian doctors.

We may conclude that thoughts and feelings are the marrow and backbone of our physical bodies. For general good health, a proper diet and exercise and fresh air are important. But 'proper diet' and 'fresh air' in thoughts and feelings are much more important.

The purpose of all great religious teachers has been to give the clue to such health of thoughts and feeling. The concept of God, the Creator and Sustainer, was a cornerstone in this mental and emotional diet. Today, nuclear physicists, astronomers and mathematicians in increasing numbers, are expressing the same general message.

The road to health of thought and feeling is the very same as the road to mental communication. A perfectly healthy mind communicates without effort. (This, of course, does not mean that a man who can so communicate is therefore healthy in all other respects.)

If we had lived in that long-past era, in the brilliant light at the surface of life, we would know, without having to be told. Now, being so far submerged, most of us have to learn. We have to be reminded and then we have to be convinced and then we must strive. Some tell us to 'concentrate', but how can we while a thousand worries scurry through our minds? We need methods.

We may take a look at ourselves, our functions, breathing, for example. What is it? Taking in fresh air? More than that. Breathing is the rhythm which links us to the space-continuum. Therefore, it is a point of attack. By linking our concentration to it, we may succeed. By putting a word, or a thought or a feeling as a weight on our breath, in or out, this word or feeling grows into our being and becomes part of us. Concentration is learned with less effort and is learned better.

There may have been a happier time, long past, when such efforts were not necessary. But today, as we are catapulted out of sleep by the jarring scream of an alarm clock and go through all the ugly disturbances of the day, we realize that we need a better feeling in the pit of the stomach. Could we but see what magic lies in wait for him who earnestly tries.

So while waiting for the next disturbance of your modern world, why not use the time for experimenting with your breathing rather than in fretting? There are many little things to explore. Breathe noiselessly. Breathe through each nostril separately. Breathe in through the mouth and out through the nose. A child who discovers and tests out his breath does such things. It may do wonders for him. And perhaps for grownups, also.

A child likes to share his play with playmates. You, a grownup, may scorn such an idea, although a nuclear physicist of my acquaintance tells me that he thinks much more clearly when he imagines that he is talking with someone who understands him perfectly. You might try to define such a friend, in terms of his loving character and his strength.

Thus, some men of old prayed, 'Beloved Lord, Almighty God, Who plays in the rays of the sun and in the waves of the air. I feel You and see You in nature and in other people and in myself...'

Even if you are not quite sure, and all this is only a suggestion to you as yet, it might be worthwhile trying it and seeing if it turns out to be true. Only those suggestions will last and produce results which are proven ultimately to be true.

He who has felt the thrill of filling his waiting time with playful breathing and magic thoughts of God, eventually becomes so fond of this game that he finds, someday, his every breath has become filled with the thought of God. Like the saints of old, he will know: 'This is not my body. It is the Temple of God.'

And he will see all other bodies as Temples of God and all other hearts as the Shrines of God. His general health, his fresh interest in life and his spurt of new energy will amaze his friends. And, in addition, he may become a seer and a knower."

"And if he is very lucky," added Edward Fitzgerald with a smile, "he may survive an Indian taxi ride."

He pointed ahead, through the murky windshield. "I do believe – and most devoutly hope – that that is your fabled city of Allahabad just ahead."

The ancient city of Allahabad is the sacred Prayag Tirtha through which three rivers flow, the Ganges, the Jumna and the Saraswati. As we entered the city, we found it a seething mass of humanity, crowded far beyond its capacity.

THE TALE OF THE MEETING OF THE RIVERS

Every twelve years, saints, sanyassins, sadhus, swamis and yogis from all over India have a meeting with Fate and the people in one of four cities: Allahabad, Hardwar, Nasik, or Ujjain. The trek to the appropriate city begins months before the great event.

In the remotest mountain regions of the Himalayas, near the Gangotry Glacier, beyond Kedernath and Badrinath in the Gharwal District, in the Nilgris or Blue Mountains of the South, and so forth, hermit saints break camp quietly and begin walking. It is a pilgrimage in reverse. In other years, millions of pilgrims trek to the holy places in the mountains to worship at the sacred shrines and to meet and listen to the hermit saints who personalize the blessed places and their histories. But in the year of the Kumbha Mela, it is the saints who go to the pilgrims. Each six years sees a smaller gathering and there is a very small one every three years, but the Kumbha Mela is unforgettable.

At a snail's pace, I forged ahead through the packed masses of humanity. Behind me, hard put not to get separated, were Edward Fitzgerald, Dr. Jacques and Sir James.

To our left was the broad Ganges, seeming about to overflow with the bulk of thousands of bathers over whom Brahmin priests performed solemn rites to enhance the spiritual blessings of their ablutions.

Parades of stern camels wormed their way through the crowds. Mighty elephants, draped in silks, lumbered past. Naked sadhus followed, waving scepters of pure gold. In the eddies and swirls of the main streams of men and beasts, in nooks and little open places along the streets, sadhus with braided hair and long beards sat cross-legged while instructing their groups of disciples and persons washed in by the movement of the turbulent stream of humanity.

Here and there, a lone yogi sat, immersed in deep meditation, oblivious to the surging life about him.

This huge and exquisite gathering was more than just a fair. There was an intangible air about it of sincerity and yearning and of sacred rites and practices. The people wore an air of happy expectation. The populace knew that, although the charlatans were also drawn to the Kumbha Mela, the really great ones, unheralded, also came. While smiling and joking and laughing, people looked searchingly and breathlessly into the faces of wild-looking yogis and exquisitely-draped sadhus. In any one of these faces might greatness be hidden. One of these men might choose suddenly to levitate, to fly up to heaven or at least to the nearest cloud.

My search was for a particular sage whom I had never met. I had only heard of him in stories told by friends more fortunate than I. Although it seemed impossible to stumble on one particular person in this astonishing mass of humanity, I had a stubborn hope for the sake of the three whom I had brought with me.

All I had promised these famous men of science were the sights and tastes and smells of the great Kumbha Mela. But they had sensed my hope that I might be able to lead them to a truly great man. I think this latter possibility was why they came. These eminent men would consider a mere fair, however huge and colorful, insufficient excuse for losing time which might be spent in their work.

Sir James Oss was the greatest physicist of our time. He had succeeded in dividing electrons, mesons, neutrons, and positrons into even smaller "particles" or "wave assemblies." In this work, he followed his fervent creed: "Forever, solid matter melts into insubstantial radiation; forever, the tangible changes into the intangible."

Dr. Jacques Miel was the beloved French founder of an international association of scientists from most, if not all, branches of science. They probed jointly into the entire field of knowledge. Every brain in the group was open and undogmatic. In the center of the web, collecting, assimilating, organizing the flow of information from the entire network sat the spider himself, Dr. Jacques. Like all true geniuses, he was accomplished in many fields, art, literature, philosophy etc. – all these expressions of his free and untrammeled soul, all contributing to the ripening of the fruits of the Centre International de Recherche Scientifique.

Edward Fitzgerald was the irrepressible American hurricane in the field of sociology. He had singlehandedly shattered the brittle structure of his country's behavioral sciences, particularly the deeply-respected concept that a three precent economic expansion in a year was all an industrially mature nation should allow, for if more is produced, what will happen to the surplus wheat and automobiles and washing machines? Fitzgerald could not see why expansion should be in things which were already in abundance. Why not shift to other things? Water desalinization, more power, cheaper power, ecology. At first, Fitzgerald's ideas were greeted with derision, but finally he was proven correct and the people who had formerly jeered at him were the loudest in lionizing him.

As we shoved our slow way along, I looked carefully at every face I could see in the niches and quiet places, comparing their features with those in my mind. To any of the three fighting their slow way along behind me, I am sure that my methods would have seemed foolish. At best, I could hope to see only a tiny fraction of all the faces of the hundreds of thousands of visitors in the city. But with childlike faith, I reasoned that if the great one I sought wished to see us, he would somehow arrange it. My task was simply to be there, available, waiting until he beckoned, if he did beckon.

Suddenly, I heard Fitzgerald's booming voice saying, "Well. Would you look at that?"

His loudness cut through the general atmosphere of devotion and awe. Sir James drew himself up and raised his eyebrows. Dr. Jacques looked baffled.

We turned toward the object of Fitzgerald's attention. It was a huge bird of the parrot family which perched on a branch of a huge eucalyptus tree. Its pink and white feathers were so bright that they seemed luminous. But the strangest thing about this bird was that it sat completely still as if in utter ecstacy, with its eyes wide open and fixed upon a human face below.

It was a face which was so radiant that it was difficult to look at its features. It was framed by silky hair which seemed to float down over his wide shoulders. The eyes were of clear, blue fire and seemed to be punching holes in the fabric of creation. This was he for whom I had searched.

Welcome. Was that word actually spoken? Or was it just a fleeting, sensed impression?

I looked at the still figure before us and then at my three silent companions who looked back at me in puzzlement.

There were four empty reed chairs set in the shadows cast by the tree, facing the sage. The four of us sat down.

"That bird," said Fitzgerald, in an unusually quiet voice. "He seems to be listening for something we can't hear."

I looked at Dr. Jacques. A luminous clarity had come over his face. He looked as though he had just become possessed of a great idea.

"You will recall," he said, "that I have meddled a bit with the Second Law of Thermodynamics. It postulates that entropy creeps up and up. This means that man and the universe are gradually going to sleep – activity is almost imperceptibly slowing down. I found, I believe, that this unfortunate trend applies only to inorganic matter and only if the inorganic matter were alone. But it is not. Life – organic matter – is there to push all and everything into waking activity again, at the right moment, with the proper force, just as a clock's mechanism gives the pendulum an upward kick at its lowest point. So the universe stays vital and may even become increasingly vital."

"That is the view of many physicists," said Sir James.

"They advocate what may be described as a cyclic universe. While it may die in one place, the products of its death are busy producing new life in other places. However, most physicists now lean toward viewing the universe as finite. Life gives the pendulum an upward kick, as you say, but only for a certain time. They believe that we are moving toward an end of time, when all will sleep. That is the Second Law of Thermodynamics. Your introduction of the life principle does not really touch that law, which applies to the inorganic area only."

"How improper," said Fitzgerald, grimacing. "The good Dr. Jacques barges into the sacred circles of the physicists and reminds them that there is life. As for Dr. Jacques, of course, he's bound to remember that. He makes his living from us, the living."

"Now here on the shores of the Ganges," continued the Frenchman, "a pleasant river breeze seems to have eased into my mind the idea of how that push of the life force is applied. The urge or wish or thought of that living thing, whether it be a man, beast, plant, germ, virus, whatever, is working, I would say, inside the electrons and protons of matter and is simply a part, in a sense, of these particles."

"Although we do now begin to split electrons into tinier wave bundles," said Sir James, "there is no sign yet that these smaller waves are thoughts or affected by thoughts."

"Quite so," said Dr. Jacques. "The thoughts or wishes are probably of a still finer order. There may be intermediary links, in order of size, between the electrons and the thoughts and feelings of the living."

"Middlemen," said Fitzgerald. "The long and tortuous

chain of command, linking thought, the commander, to the electrons and protons – the soldiers or workers – just as in any long-winded, frustratingly bureaucratic sociological pattern."

"Far-fetched, but challenging," said Sir James. "You are in distinguished company, you know. Many physicists today look at the universe, not as a machine or a biologist's dream, but as a product of pure thought, or pure mathematics. Everything appears to have ultimately been made of thought, forged and held by a master thinker. You say that these thoughts are wave clusters deeply hidden inside the electrons and the protons? Why not? If it could be given mathematical expression – why not, indeed?"

"All right, Sir James," said Fitzgerald. "You provide the equations. We sociologists will translate them into law, economics, international relations and sex."

"My metallic catalyzers," said Dr. Jacques, "indicate that the wave characteristics of the gold and silver atoms facilitate and greatly improve many of the functions of the patient's body and of his thoughts."

"If electrons and protons are directed by living thoughts and wishes," mused Fitzgerald, "who are the super-wishers and thinkers who create and operate this universe? If it were subject to the whims of the ordinary sort of person, the whole thing would blow up or just dissolve."

"Physicists," said Sir James, "are recapturing and streamlining the ancient idea about a masterful Creator. His is the mind which keeps the universe intact."

"And the East-West tension? And the Chinese invasion of Tibet?" said Fitzgerald bitterly.

"Ah," said Dr. Jacques. "Now we are coming to the humans. In the ancient books, you know, they speak of a Creator making man from clay in His own image. Man, then, would be a microcosmos compared with the macrocosmos. The microcosmos, of course, is closely related to the big universe, but cannot bring any influence to bear on it until he learns the secrets of his own micro-existence. Before we discover these secrets, we fool about whimsically, amusing ourselves with invasions and East-West tensions. When the day comes when we know how to influence and dissolve and reshape the atoms of our own bodies and minds, through knowing the laws and obeying the laws and through constant practice, then and only then, I think, will we be able to gradually influence the universe. By then we will be dependable and sensible enough, I hope, not to explode or dissolve the world before its time."

"In physics," said Sir James thoughtfully, "we often use the expression that an electron must, in a certain sense, occupy the whole of the universe. In other words, it exerts its influence everywhere and it is influenced from everywhere, even from human thought. We don't know, however, whether human thought is a primary or even a strong influence. We do know that everything and everybody is linked to everything and everybody else. The linking, as we understand it, happens through radiation, the masses of which are exceedingly small, compared to the masses of matter."

"Which simply means to me," said Dr. Jacques, "that great powers of actual or potential radiation are bound up in matter."

"If weight is a criterion," said Sir James, "then a bar

of lead might be more powerful than my whole body."

Dr. Jacques shook his head. "No. The bar of lead may have mighty powers because of sheer mass, but when viewed in relation to the latent powers in a living human body, I think the heaviest bar could be called a stunted dwarf. Life adds a new dimension."

"That's comforting to know," said Sir James with a smile.

Dr. Jacques continued, "A bar of lead may release its energy into an explosion or release it slowly and drive an engine. A living being can, in addition, plan and build and pilot a jet-liner. When a complete master of his powers, I would guess that he could build palaces from atoms or turn castles into dust or keep a million enemies at bay while turning them into friends. He could, in effect, at least, change the course of the world."

"You've comforted me, too," said Fitzgerald. "I like to think that my body is mightier than the heap of atomic dirt which has been running the Sea Wolf for years."

"Potentially," said Dr. Jacques.

I looked at the silent member of our group who sat cross-legged before us. Was he inspiring this conversation? Was he performing as an orchestra leader, directing with rays of thoughts for a baton? If so, the highly intuitive Dr. Jacques was his first violin, Sir James the deep and solid cello bass. Edward Fitzgerald, the whole tympanic section. And what was I? Absolutely nothing, I realized. Only the one who brought them all together – the public relations man. That was all.

Suddenly the scene expanded before my inner vision. I saw the eminent Yogi continuing the concert and his conducting from his retreat in the Himalayas, for a lifetime or more, now that he had made contact. Or did the concert actually extend backward in time, also? Had he already been guiding the thoughts of these and other persons from his distant abode? Had he just arranged this meeting as a pleasant break in routine or to cement the relationship?

The great one was obviously not going to give me answers to these questions — why should he? Who was I to warrant even a glance? At the moment my mind formulated the question, his eyes, full and blue and penetrating, fell on me. I realized with an unspoken apology that I already had the answer.

I began to listen to Dr. Jacques once more. "...and that my catalyzers, to my friends and myself," he was saying, "were only a first and clumsy step along the way. Our next step, we all thought, would be some machine or device which threw the desired waves into the affected body part directly. And the next and final stage would be for the patient to direct his own mastered thought or feeling to the affected spot in such a way that proper wave activity and, hence, health, would be restored."

"Some here in India are suppose do be able to do that already, you know," said Fitzgerald.

"So I have heard," said Dr. Jacques. "And whether there really are such persons now or not, especially gifted individuals would certainly precede the general accomplishments and serve as healers of others until the majority came around."

"You poor pill-peddler," taunted Fitzgerald, "then how would you make a living?"

"Wouldn't have to, that's the beauty of it!"

"And I presume…" Sir James had an edge to his voice, "that the command of inorganic atoms would allow man to create his houses and clothing directly from thought forms?"

""With your assistance, yes," said the doctor, "although shelter and clothing might be superfluous when heat and cold would be mastered through the body processes."

"Afraid there would be boringly little to do in such a civilization…"

"Except for research into the never-ending mystery of things and men!"

"Hm, yes," admitted Sir James, "that's right. What, for example, might be beyond thought? Wouldn't those tiny wave bundles be divisible into still smaller bundles? Where would this division end, if ever? Would we finally be able to mathematically define soul – and God?"

We sat there without talking, each with his own thoughts. Then, a shuffling of feet. We rose to leave. Fitzgerald glanced back, not at the bird this time, but at the sage.

"The great one who got away, why, he wasn't any trouble at all!"

THE END

Acknowledgements

This edition of *Fairy Tales are True* has been published as it was originally written by Shamcher Bryn Beorse in the late 1960s and early 1970s with very few editorial changes. The subtitle, chapter headings and an introduction have been added to this original work.

We are grateful to Diane Feught for her insightful cover design and to Joe Clare, patron of the arts and humanity, for his support for the production of this edition.

Thanks are also due to Norm Hammond, author of *The Dunites* and *Elwood Decker, Spirit of the Dunes*, for verifying some of the details in this volume and for his continued inspiring work as historian of the Oceano Dunes.

Fairy Tales are True: Silent Reach from the Dunes to the Kumbha Mela is a publication of the Shamcher Archives, dedicated to preserving and publishing the works of Shamcher Bryn Beorse. It was previously published in 1978 by Hu Press, NY, with original cover art by Qayyum Michael Brain.

Find background to the book, original cover image, reference links, and further details at:

www.fairy-tales.shamcher.com

About the Author

Bryn Beorse (Shamcher) (1896-1980) was the author of many non-fiction books, novels and articles, covering topics of energy, economics, full employment, and global awareness as well as yoga and Sufism.

Born in Norway, he worked and travelled in over 65 countries in his lifetime, and he eventually settled in the United States. Fluent in several languages, his comprehensive worldview included the inner meditative life as well as the accomplishment of life in the world. Sent on a UN economic mission to Tunisia in the 1960's, helping to rebuild the Norwegian economy after WWII, Beorse also spent time in exploration, travelling to the Kumbha Mela in India, living as a beach bum in the dunes of Oceano, and going to China at the time of the revolution. A spy in WWII, he was part of the plot to kidnap Hitler. An advocate of the giro-credit economic system, he spoke out against the stagnation of hierarchical organization.

An accomplished yogi and Sufi, Shamcher was instrumental in developing Sufi centres throughout the world, in the tradition of Inayat Khan. He dedicated the last years of his life to OTEC, Ocean Thermal Energy Conversion, a source of benign solar power from the sea.

More info at: www.shamcher.org